THE SUCCESSFUL TEACHER'S GUIDE TO FREQUENTLY ASKED QUESTIONS

SALLY C. MAYBERRY
LYNN HARTLE

A SCARECROWEDUCATION BOOK

The Scarecrow Press, Inc.
Lanham, Maryland, and Oxford
2003

A SCARECROWEDUCATION BOOK

Published in the United States of America
by Scarecrow Press, Inc.
A wholly owned subsidiary of The Rowman & Littlefield Publishing Group, Inc.
4501 Forbes Boulevard, Suite 200, Lanham, MD 20706 ·
www.scarecroweducation.com

PO Box 317
Oxford
OX2 9RU, UK

British Library Cataloguing in Publication Information Available

Library of Congress Cataloging-in-Publication Data

Mayberry, Sally Cox, 1937–
    The successful teacher's guide to frequently asked questions / Sally
C. Mayberry, Lynn Hartle.
        p. cm.
    "A ScarecrowEducation book."
    Includes bibliographical references and index.
    ISBN 0-8108-4763-9 (pbk. : alk. paper)
    1. Elementary school teaching—Handbooks, manuals, etc. 2. Teacher
effectiveness—Handbooks, manuals, etc. I. Hartle, Lynn, 1955– II.
Title.
LB1555.M423 2003
371.1102—dc21

                                        2003001745

∞™ The paper used in this publication meets the minimum requirements of
American National Standard for Information Sciences—Permanence of
Paper for Printed Library Materials, ANSI/NISO Z39.48-1992.
Manufactured in the United States of America.

CONTENTS

INTRODUCTION

A t the conclusion of the inservice, several teachers gathered by the presenter. One commented, "That was great! I have always had questions about cooperative grouping and you showed me how to go about using it. I can't wait to share these ideas with my team."

This comment and others led these authors to believe that a real need exists to "get the information out" about issues and trends in the field of education. We know, having both been primary and elementary teachers ourselves, that time is of the essence. Each teacher must juggle schedules, conferences, curriculum planning, always choosing what is best for the children. Most school schedules leave little time for planning. Reading professional literature must take place in the evening and on weekends. A source book for quick information could provide the motivation to get new projects underway or curricular changes implemented.

Teachers, like university personnel, are being asked to take on greater roles in school reform efforts and curriculum development. All of these new roles mandate the gathering of current, effective research information.

This book can be used as a quick reference for teachers seeking the why's and how's for implementation of new educational trends. A section can be read quickly while stuck in traffic, waiting for the dentist, or in between meetings. Follow-up is quickly available in the resources section at the end of each chapter. The topics written here were selected specifically for use by primary and elementary teachers, but can be applied in preK–8 classrooms with minor adjustments.

1

ACTION RESEARCH

In November, Mr. Redfeather realized that children in his first grade at Eagle Ridge Elementary had the widest range of math skills he had ever noticed during his three years of teaching. The other two first-grade teachers also commented on students' wide range of skills and knowledge. Some children were still working on making sets of numbers one through ten, while others understood and could perform some simple multiplication problems. Still others were somewhere in between in this continuum of development and could perform simple addition problems by using manipulative materials. That year, Mr. Redfeather had a university intern, Ms. Black, who had an assignment to conduct action research. He considered the intern's project an excellent opportunity to study some changes he had planned to make in his teaching to accommodate children's diverse needs. When Mr. Redfeather told the other two first-grade teachers at Eagle Ridge about action research, they wanted to be a part of the project, too.

WHAT IS MEANT BY ACTION RESEARCH?

Action research is a disciplined inquiry undertaken by educators and other practitioners in order that they may improve their own practices. It is a systematic, reflective, and collaborative process used to examine practices and individuals for the purposes of planning change (Calhoun, 2002; Hopkins, 2002; Hubbard & Power, 1993; Jarvis, 1998).

The essential characteristics of action research include the following:

- Practitioners select questions about teaching strategies that aren't working or strategies they want to try out and that they choose to study.
- Much of the data collection and analysis are done by the practitioners in their own classrooms, but study teams may also include interns, university partners, principals, and other practitioners.

Sometimes a teacher works alone to study his or her own practice, or teachers collaborate such as on the project with the first-grade teachers and university intern at Eagle Ridge. The principal at Eagle Ridge was eager to see the results of the first-grade team's collaborative efforts to accommodate a wide range of learners. Collaborative research can also extend to teachers and classrooms across the entire school or several schools (Anderson, Herr, & Nihlen, 1994; Calhoun, 2002; Glanz, 1998; McLean, 1995).

WHAT ARE SOME ADVANTAGES AND CONCERNS TO CONDUCTING ACTION RESEARCH?

- Teachers can investigate their own teaching in ways they prefer to improve children's learning, thus being motivated by ownership in the teaching-learning process.
- If solutions to the needs of children in the class are found through cooperating with other teachers, the end results are usually better than if one teacher had conducted the research in isolation.
- Teachers learn systematic data collection about teaching and learning.
- Teachers who collaborate with others in the research gain peer support beyond what they usually have, because classroom teaching can be isolating.

There may be some doubts or challenges to conducting action research, such as:

- Teachers may feel that they have a lack of skills to be able to conduct the study.

- Teachers may feel threatened, initially, when they have to juxtapose their own current practices against multiple sources of data and readings about others' exemplar research-based practices.
- Teachers may feel that time to collect data could take away from instructional time, so they can develop creative ways for children's work to be part of the performance assessment of each child.
- Teachers may not know how to get started.

HOW DO I BEGIN AN ACTION RESEARCH PROJECT?

Throughout the action research process, staff development may be required for teachers to gain needed skills or knowledge. The principal or curriculum coordinator may bring in experts on the selected subject or teachers in the building who have specialized skills may conduct the staff development.

Start with a good problem statement or questions about teaching that can be focused by:

- Keeping a journal of what is currently done to prepare for, for example, math lessons and learning processes each child used during lessons.
- Brainstorming a list of things you wondered about or specific concerns.
- Considering—Who is affected? Who or what is suspected of causing the problem?
- Considering what is expected of children to learn and do—family, school, state, and your own expectations.
- Determining what the internal school factors that may contribute to this problem, for example, programs, initiatives, instructional practices, are.
- Determining what the external school factors that contribute to this problem, for example, how the school is rated compared to other schools, district or statewide mandates, are.
- Having teachers develop a draft question. Further fine tuning can narrow the question to allow teachers to more fully study one problem or concern at a time. In the example, above, the first-grade teachers' questions were: "How can the existing mandated math curriculum be adapted to

accommodate the range of learners in our first-grade class to ensure all children achieve the required first-grade competencies while others can be challenged at higher levels according to their abilities? Further, how can these math experiences be relevant to children's lives?"

The first-grade teachers and intern in the above example then gathered resources to help them solve the problem by: reading one or two relevant articles or books based on their questions; and involving other teachers or the principal to provide support or encouragement.

The next step is to gather data. The most important tool you have as a researcher is your eye and your view of classroom life. You will have the opportunity to look deeply at yourself and your students' work. What you see around you is data. Other tools/instruments you may use to gather data include: checklists of expected concept development, interviews of children/families, anecdotal records of children at work, samples of student work, teacher-made tests, studies of who plays/works with whom (sociograms), and audio/videotapes.

Good guidelines for data collection include:

- The instruments should measure what the tools suggest they will.
- The instruments should measure the information researchers need to solve the problem.
- Collect just enough data—not too much, not too little.

Good times to gather data include:

- at the beginning of class before lessons;
- during independent or small group work times; and after school.

Hint: Develop collection systems, such as color-coded baskets so children can help you gather their own work for teacher analysis.

HOW DO I ORGANIZE AND ANALYZE THE DATA?

The following are examples of how Mr. Redfeather and Ms. Black analyzed their data:

- They made multiple passes (repeated readings) through transcriptions of videotapes and interviews to look for key impressions, affective impressions, content, for example, one index card made for each new pattern realized, such as children who liked to work with beads, and another card for children partners who worked well together, and another card for questions the teacher asked that provoked some children to extend their thinking.
- They recorded the types of errors each child made on his or her papers.
- They developed case studies of each child's selected behaviors, work, or actions based on interviews and observations during center time.
- Validity is established through triangulation (the sharing of ideas with others who collaborate), such as the intern and other colleagues in other classes who chose to study their math classes. Triangulation is also established by using more than one data source (such as these teachers' use of interviews, videotapes) to avoid biasing with minimal information from one source.

Recurring Cycles of Data Collection and Analysis

After you find out what kinds of situations improve learning, try making changes in your teaching or environment and continue to collect data about those improvements. Your action research never has to end and can continue as teacher reflection and revision of practices can be ongoing.

How Do I Use and Report Findings?

- The teacher and children can, together, use the research findings/information to make learning experiences more effective for the diverse range of learners in classrooms.
- Teachers can choose to write up their findings for an article for a journal or newsletter.
- Teachers can conduct a staff development workshop on processes used and/or findings for other teachers.
- Create a fact sheet or "white paper."

WHAT ARE SOME FREQUENTLY ASKED QUESTIONS ABOUT CONDUCTING ACTION RESEARCH?

1. How much time is needed?

Action research can last as little as a few weeks to several years depending on the depth of the study or questions to be answered. School-wide action research takes a longer period of time as teachers must first develop rapport and develop some mutually agreed upon research questions before conducting any research.

2. How much background reading of articles or books is needed by teachers?

Some reading of new methods or theories about teaching and learning is very important to rejuvenate or spark new ideas or ways of thinking about teaching that can be studied. Teachers who collaborate on the research can divide up reading assignments and come together at designated times for readings discussions. Continually reading throughout the research study keeps the "juices flowing" and the excitement level high.

3. Can families of the children be involved in the action research?

Families should be part of the entire process so they can take part in the spirit of rejuvenation. Some family members may even help with data collection.

4. What are some conditions that support schoolwide action research?

A majority of the teachers and administrators must be willing to change. Some may want to "wait and see" what happens while another class tries the innovation first.

CONCLUSION: HOW CAN YOU CONTINUE THE INQUIRY CYCLE?

Build data gathering, organizing, analyzing into your daily routine. Teach the children to help you keep records and portfolios. Above all—have fun with your exploration of learning and teaching.

RESOURCES

Anderson, G., Herr, K., & Nihlen, A. S. (1994). *Studying Your Own School: An Educator's Guide to Qualitative Practitioner Research.* Thousand Oaks, CA: Corwin Press. Administrators and curriculum resource teachers will find this a helpful resource for implementing action research in classrooms throughout the school.

Bevevino, M. M. & Snodgrass, D. M. (2000). Action Research in the Classroom: Increasing the Comfort Zone. *Clearinghouse, 73*(5): 254–58. (ERIC #EJ604772). Through action research, a group of teachers analyzed a variety of ways assessments affect the quality of their teaching.

Borgia, E. T. & Schuler, D. (1996). *Action Research in Early Childhood Education.* (ERIC Digest. EDO-PS-96-11). This concise resource has tips for both early childhood and elementary school teachers and makes a great handout to first introduce action research to other teachers.

Calhoun, E. F. (2002). Action Research for School Improvement. *Educational Leadership, 59*(6): 18–23. Teachers and administrators in this article share the profound professional change their schools experience when regular use of multiple sources of data inform their practices and improve student learning.

Glanz, J. (1998). *Action Research: An Educational Leader's Guide to School Improvement.* Norwood, MA: Christopher-Gordon. This book takes the administrator's perspective on how action research can be conducted and used to support total school improvement.

Hopkins, D. (2002). *A Teacher's Guide to Classroom Research* (3rd ed.). Buckingham, England: Open University Press. This practical guide of specifics for conducting action research is for teachers who wish to improve classroom practice through the study of their own teaching but also includes strategies for whole school improvement.

Hubbard, R. S. & Power, B. M. (1993). *The Art of Classroom Inquiry: A Handbook for Teacher-Researchers.* Portsmouth, NH: Heineman. Almost a step-by-step manual for conducting and using action research, this resource is especially helpful for teachers to develop thoughtful research questions.

Jarvis, P. (1998). *The Practitioner-Researcher: Developing Theory from Practice.* San Francisco: Jossey-Bass. Beyond tools for action research, this book uses case studies of teachers who study their own practice to bridge the theories of research with practice.

McLean, J. (1995). *Improving Education through Action Research: A Guide for Administrators and Teachers.* The Practicing Administrator's Leadership Series: Roadmaps to Success. Thousand Oaks, CA: Corwin Press. Another school reform resource, this guide is part of a series of books for administrators.

CHILDREN WITH SPECIAL NEEDS

A child is first a child regardless of any learning or social disabilities or delays. Each child is also unique and therefore special in some ways.

WHAT IS MEANT BY CHILDREN WITH SPECIAL NEEDS?

Even professionals vary in their definitions of typical or normal development rather than atypical development or special needs of children. Many children who are diagnosed as having special needs resemble children who are typically developing in more ways than they differ from them.

In fact, the fields of special education and general education are moving away from categorical definitions of children's special needs and special talents, respecting a "people first" approach. The term *handicapped* is becoming less acceptable. Rather than focusing on a person's deficit that highlights a problem or talent first, the phrase "children with special needs" highlights the child first. For example, considering a "child with learning disabilities" (rather than as a "learning disabled" child) puts the individual child's needs and interests at the forefront.

WHAT ARE SOME ADVANTAGES AND CONCERNS RELATED TO DEFINING CHILDREN'S SPECIAL NEEDS?

Despite the efforts to move away from a categorical system that labels children with a specific disability, in order to secure funding to serve children who have special needs, some identification measured by appropriate diagnostic instruments and procedures is needed. Young children age three to nine are eligible for services if they have been diagnosed with behaviors outside of the typical range of expected development or *developmental delays* in the areas of physical development, cognitive development, communication development, social or emotional development, or adaptive development. Some children with delays may be at risk for serious problems (especially those who live in poverty or have experienced some trauma in-utero or during birthing). The intent is that early intervention may prevent later problems. Children who in their early years had *developmental delays* can be prepared for schools and services with children who are typically developing. Children should be served as early as possible, that is, as infants and young children.

Children (ages birth to twenty-one) who have been diagnosed with specific learning disabilities, speech/language impairments, mental retardation, serious emotional disturbance, multiple disabilities, hearing impairments, orthopedic impairments, other health impairments, visual impairments, autism, deaf-blindness, and traumatic brain injury (listed in the order of number of children served in the United States, highest to lowest) are eligible for a cascade of services dependent on the severity of their disabilities. Children may have multiple special needs and the level of severity of each need may vary from mild to moderate to severe. Attempting to label a child with one label may provide a misunderstanding of that child's full range of needs and talents.

Children with special gifts and talents may require special services; those who seem to be more advanced in one or more areas of development, that is, mathematics, language arts, or visual or performing arts. Some children with special talents may also have a developmental disability, such as a hearing impairment. Some districts and schools serve children with special talents in special classrooms all day or certain days of the school week, while other schools provide enrichment within the regular classroom. More recently some schools are considering ALL children's multiple intelligences (see chapter 11) rather than a narrow view of only mathematical or language talents. Schools are then adapting and individualizing curriculums to challenge and support children to achieve their personal best.

HOW DO I BEGIN SERVING CHILDREN WITH SPECIAL NEEDS?

The Individuals with Disabilities Education Act (IDEA), Public Law 94-142, newly reauthorized in 1997 as IDEA (defined later in this chapter) provides legal supports and definitions for children with special needs and their families. Central to the law is that a study team of professionals (i.e., special education teacher, general education teacher, physical therapist, occupational therapist) and each child's family work as a team to plan services for each child with special needs. Through their collaborative planning, an Individualized Education Plan (IEP) is developed with short-term and annual goals and teaching strategies and therapy tailored for that child. Some parts of a child's plan may detail services to be received while in classes with peers who are typically developing, one-on-one at home or school, or in small groups. Each child's IEP is to be based on valid and nondiscriminatory assessment and should be modified on a regular basis with updated regular assessment. Basic sections of the IEP are: present level of functioning, annual goals, short-term objectives, special services, beginning and duration of services, and evaluation.

A cascade of services are available to children and should be the least restrictive (as similar as possible to services for children who are typically developing and whenever possible with children who are typically developing). Services should be specific to the severity (mild, moderate, or severe) and type of each child's special needs (i.e., hearing impairment, physical-motor impairment) and should consider each family's wishes. For some children with severe special needs or very young children, home care or group home care meets their needs. Most elementary age children with special needs are provided services in public school settings while some preschool-age children are served in private preschools or Head Start centers.

One school-based appropriate setting might be a self-contained classroom including children with Varying Exceptionalities (VE), children with various diagnosed special needs (i.e., visually impaired and mild mental retardation) or developmental delays. Self-contained classes for children, all with the same disability (such as those with hearing impairments), is another possible placement. Children may spend only a small part of their day in special needs classes. While children may be placed in special education classes, it is important to realize children may be similar to or vary in abilities in the same ways as their typically developing peers. Full or partial inclusion (see chapter 9) of children with special needs in classrooms with their typically developing peers depends on the child study team's decision of the most appropriate and least restrictive environment.

WHAT ARE SOME FREQUENTLY ASKED QUESTIONS ABOUT SERVING CHILDREN WITH SPECIAL NEEDS?

1. What are the causes (etiology) of special needs and talents?

Causes of special needs and talents vary and can occur before the child is born, during the birthing process, or any time during childhood or adolescent years. Much less is known regarding the causes for talents, but research has uncovered links to both genetics and enriched early and later experiences for children with talents. Some of the causes for developmental disabilities include: genetics of parents, chromosomal disorders occurring during the conception and gene recombination process causing a syndrome (i.e., Down's syndrome), metabolic disorders (i.e., Tay-Sachs), parental infections during pregnancy (i.e., rubella), and environmental (i.e., maternal use of drugs and alcohol).

2. What are the major laws governing services?

Passed in 1975, the most notable law that for the first time guaranteed all children and youth, regardless of the severity of the disability, a free and appropriate public education is the *Education for All Handicapped Children*

Act, signed into PL 94-142. No child may be rejected (zero reject) from receiving services in the local school district. This law provides for strong family involvement in the process of both assessing and serving their children. Under this law, children are entitled to full individual testing specific to their cultural and language needs. All children must be then provided with education appropriate to each child's special needs. To the greatest extent possible children with special needs must be educated in settings alongside their typically developing peers and with the supports they need. And to ensure all of this is in place, families have legal right of due process—to call a special meeting if they don't agree with the school district's educational decisions for their children.

In 1986, Congress passed the Education of the Handicapped Amendments, P.L. 99-457. This law clarified and redefined services for infants, toddlers, and preschool children illustrating commitment to early intervention as the best way to improve the quality of life for children with developmental disabilities.

P.L. 94-142 was reauthorized in 1990 and renamed the Individuals with Disabilities Act (IDEA). The law was reauthorized again in 1997 to provide stronger support against segregated services for children and youth with disabilities (see http://www.ideapractices.org/law/regulations/index.php). In 1990, the Americans with Disabilities Act (ADA), P.L. 101-336, was passed to provide civil rights protection to individuals. This law provided for appropriate physical, telecommunications, and transportation access in private employment.

3. How can I learn more about specific special needs?

The following selected organizations that are available to help teachers and families include:

- The Association for Retarded Citizens (ARC), an advocacy group www.thearc.org;
- The Council for Exceptional Children (CEC), the largest international professional organization dedicated to improving educational outcomes for individuals with exceptionalities, students with disabilities, and/or the gifted www.cec.sped.org;
- National Information Center for Children and Youth with Disabilities (NICHCY), some services include providing information and making

referrals in areas related to specific disabilities, early intervention, special education and related services, and individualized education programs http://www.nichcy.org/; and

- Child Find, a federal program established in the 1960s, with local offices in communities across the United States to locate children in need of special services.

CONCLUSION

Services for children with special needs continue to change since PL 94-142 was enacted in 1975. Contemporary research provides new insights into early intervention and effective accommodation strategies. Family and social service efforts have also increased public awareness surrounding least restrictive services for children with special needs. While the quality and extent of services for children with special needs has come a long way since 1975, professionals and families find continued advocacy efforts are necessary for appropriate services for ALL children.

RESOURCES

Batshaw, M. L. (Ed.). (2002). *Children with Disabilities* (5th ed.). Baltimore, MD: Paul H. Brookes. This comprehensive book provides strategies and case studies of family, developmental, educational, and clinical issues surrounding children with special needs.

Hallahan, D. P. & Kauffman, J. M. (2003). *Exceptional Learners: Introduction to Special Education* (9th ed.). Boston, MA: Allyn & Bacon. This is a popular book because of its clear descriptions of practical strategies for teaching children with special needs.

Mayberry, S. C. & Lazarus, B. B. (2002). *Teaching Students with Special Needs in the 21st Century Classroom.* Lanham, MD: Scarecrow Press. This book provides quick answers for teachers wishing to create successful inclusive classrooms.

Smith, D. D. (2001). *Introduction to Special Education: Teaching in an Age of Opportunity* (4th ed.). Boston, MA: Allyn & Bacon. This survey book of special education attends to the needs of linguistically and culturally diverse children with special needs and provides strategies for partnerships with families.

Thurlow, M. L. & Krentz, J. L. (2001). A New Vision for Special Education Accountability. *The State Education Standard, 2*(3), 4–7. This article presents the research and practices of states that include children with special needs in standards-based assessments under certain conditions to ensure children with disabilities are held to the same standards as their typically developing peers.

Turnbull, A. P., Shank, M., Smith, S., Leal, D., & Tu, R. (2001). *Exceptional Lives: Special Education in Today's Schools* (3rd ed.). Upper Saddle River, NJ: Pearson Education, Inc. This book provides an overview of the contemporary field of special education.

CLASSROOM MANAGEMENT

The effective classroom teacher prepares and organizes the classroom with the same amount of effort as that spent on implementing the curriculum. Classroom management is a critical issue in classrooms all around the country. National polls continually reveal that discipline is a major concern in schools, and discipline is a large part of classroom management. The term *classroom management*, however, includes far more than maintaining discipline in the classroom.

WHAT IS MEANT BY CLASSROOM MANAGEMENT?

The effective teacher should create a positive classroom environment that promotes learning (Stronge, 2002). Creating a positive learning environment involves classroom routines, the way a teacher relates to the class, activities to discover how students feel about the class, and more. Classroom management incorporates all of a teacher's responsibilities and activities that provide student motivation and involvement in the learning process to create a positive working environment. It includes understanding the importance of student participation in creating classroom rules, promoting positive relationships between peers and between teacher/students, and providing problem-solving techniques to encourage learning and avoid/resolve behavior problems.

Jere Brophy's (1988) definition of classroom management summarizes it well. Good classroom management implies not only that the teacher has elicited the cooperation of the students in minimizing misconduct and can intervene effectively when misconduct occurs, but also that worthwhile academic activities are occurring more or less continuously. Classroom management systems as a whole (which includes, but is not limited to the teacher's disciplinary interventions) is designed to maximize student engagement in those activities, not merely to minimize misconduct (p. 3).

WHAT ARE THE ADVANTAGES AND CONCERNS ABOUT CLASSROOM MANAGEMENT?

Teachers are continually asked to instruct a wide variety of students with differing abilities, emotional problems, and interpersonal skills (see chapter 18). Many teachers, though, have received little or no training in classroom organization and management. Research suggests that teachers who perceive classroom management as a process of setting up and furthering an effective learning environment may appear to be more successful than those who rule more strictly (Good and Brophy, 2002). Kounin's (1970) renowned study illustrates that the key to classroom management is the implementation of techniques that encourage student involvement and cooperation rather than those that allow problems to develop and increase. He found that the teachers who minimized disruptions by resolving minor incidents before they erupted into major problems modeled the most effective classroom management.

One primary concern is that classroom management strategies are not often included as part of teacher training nor included in recertification programs. Knowledge of content is important, but knowledge of classroom management skills is equally important to enable the students' learning of that content.

HOW DO I BEGIN?

There are numerous books written on the subject of effective classroom management (see Resources, this chapter). The list that follows, though not inclusive, will help teachers address many of the concepts of effective class-room management. One of the most important details is to start the school year with a well-organized plan. Preplanning at the beginning of the school year cannot be overemphasized.

WHAT ARE SOME FREQUENTLY ASKED QUESTIONS ABOUT CLASSROOM MANAGEMENT?

1. What is an effective classroom management plan for classroom procedures and routines?

An effective classroom management plan should include the following (provided in random order):

- Involve students in creating a short list of classroom procedures and routines.
- Plan transition times between subjects and between activities carefully.
- Communicate assignments and procedures clearly and effectively.
- Create a poster stating "What to do when there is nothing to do" for reference when assignments are completed.
- Implement a varied, yet challenging, schedule to promote active involvement.
- Model procedures for students to sharpen pencils, obtain your help, and/or your attention.
- Practice the correct way to enter and leave the classroom and to begin class each day.
- Provide procedures for obtaining/returning materials and for heading papers.
- Practice procedures for coming in late, leaving early, or returning to class after an absence.
- Carefully institute the use of "wait time." Wait longer than three seconds after posing a question to give students time to think of a response.
- Discuss and practice the acceptable fire drill behaviors and required routes.

- Issue "one-minute warnings" immediately prior to clean-up time to allow students to bring closure to an activity.
- Rotate the use of individual, small-group, and large-group activities to maintain a high level of student interest.

2. What is an effective classroom management plan for assignments?

- Hold positive, high-level yet realistic expectations of all students.
- Maximize instructional time to limit disruptions.
- Use meaningful, quality academic activities.
- Overplan . . . always have a Plan B and C.
- Promote understanding of academic concepts.
- Hands-on activities promote learning in a special way—implement them often.

3. What is an effective classroom management plan for classroom behaviors?

- Respect each student.
- Plan time to learn about your students as individuals.
- Constantly monitor the class for signs of inattention.
- Follow through on consequences for misbehavior (be consistent).
- Use positive language.
- Praise effectively and specifically.
- Implement strategies to gain and hold student attention.
- Model ways to deal with class interruptions.
- Promote self-discipline in the students.
- Remember that a touch of humor brings joy to the day.
- Enthusiasm is contagious . . . share yours!

4. What should I do next?

Start a collection of articles and ideas on effective classroom management plans from your peers and from professional journals, books, and websites. Store these ideas in a brightly colored folder at the front of a filing cabinet in your classroom for easy access. One can *never* have *too many* effective classroom management ideas.

CONCLUSION

An investment of time in order to establish cohesive rules, routines, and procedures early in the school year can reap rich rewards as the year progresses. Implementing effective classroom management strategies is a necessary part of planning for a successful year. Plan early, plan well, and be consistent.

RESOURCES

Brophy, J. (1988). Educating Teachers about Managing Classrooms and Students. *Teachers and Teacher Education, 4*(1), 1–18.

Good, T. L. & Brophy, J. E. (2002). *Looking in Classrooms.* New York: Addison Wesley Longman. This is a teacher-friendly book that includes chapters on preventing classroom problems and on coping effectively when problems occur.

Jones, V. F. & Jones, L. S. (2001). *Comprehensive Classroom Management: Creating Communities of Support and Solving Problems.* Boston: Allyn and Bacon. A must for every educator's library, this book provides positive answers to classroom management concerns as well as how to deal positively with parents.

Kellough, R. D. (1996). *Integrating Mathematics and Science for Intermediate and Middle School Students.* Englewood Cliffs, NJ: Prentice Hall. The chapter on classroom issues and concerns included here is an excellent resource for teachers.

Kounin, J. (1970). *Discipline and Group Management in Classrooms.* New York: Holt, Rinehart and Winston. A classic book, this includes findings on what works best in effective classrooms.

Nelsen, J., Escobar, L., Ortolano, K., Duffy, R., & Owen-Sohocki, D. (2001). *Positive Discipline: A Teacher's A–Z Guide.* Roseville, CA: Prima Publishers (Random House). Covering a multitude of current topics for the classroom teacher, this book offers short chapters on A–Z topics such as homework, lunchroom behavior, and parent communication.

Stronge, J. H. (2002). *Qualities of Effective Teachers.* Alexandria, VA: Association for Supervision and Curriculum Development. Chapters 3, 4, and 5 address important issues on classroom management and the organization and implementation of instruction.

Wong, H. K. & Wong, R. (1998). *The First Days of School: How to Be an Effective Teacher.* Mountain View, CA: Harry K. Wong Publications. This book is geared to address the new teacher and how to achieve success from the very first day in the classroom.

CONFLICT RESOLUTION

C onflict appears to be a given part of everyday life in the community and in the schools. There are, however, many ways to resolve conflict. One can choose to flee, fight, go to court, or numerous other options in between.

Fundamental to resolving conflict is realizing that conflict is normal and natural and that interpersonal and intergroup conflicts can be solved through constructive problem solving. In fact, students can come to consider conflict as a source of learning and self-understanding as they work through problems. Everyone can profit from learning conflict resolution skills.

WHAT IS MEANT BY CONFLICT RESOLUTION?

Generally speaking, conflict resolution refers to strategies that enable students to handle conflicts that occur in the classroom or school peacefully and cooperatively. The skills and processes often considered as conflict resolution include negotiation, mediation, peer mediation, and collaborative problem solving. Conflict resolution is grounded in cooperative problem solving between individuals; however, the resolution of a problem is not always a compromise of either or both persons' ideas or positions. Resolution is more often a decision all persons in the conflict can accept. More important is identifying the underlying needs of those involved in a conflict to find a solution that is lasting and meaningful and reduce the chance of future conflicts.

WHAT ARE THE ADVANTAGES AND CONCERNS ABOUT THE USE OF CONFLICT RESOLUTION?

In contemporary society, teaching conflict resolution skills may be one of our most important tasks. In this high-technology world of stress in which we live, we need a generation of problem solvers who can handle problems in a productive manner. Students, teachers, and administrators working together to solve problems can become a common goal.

To operate effectively in the social world, students must learn to recognize, interpret, and respond to social situations. They must also make judgments about how to reconcile differences between their own needs and interests and the demands and expectations of the social environments in which they live. Every day, conflicts can arise as children experience differences in others' values and interests or the context of limited resources. They are put to the test of using whatever skills they possess to resolve conflict. How well they resolve conflict is a measure of their social competence (Kostelnik, Stein, Whiren, & Soderman, 1993).

A growing number of children in this country experience threats to their psychological and physical safety that impede healthy competence in their social world. These children may be surrounded by verbal or physical violence in their daily lives and on TV and they have learned to use violence to resolve conflict. Conflict resolution programs can provide lifelong alternatives to violence.

Conflict resolution programs have been proven successful when students show more positive attitudes toward conflict and more often choose to engage in problem solving rather than win-lose negotiations. As a result, students are referred less often to the principal.

Training for conflict resolution programs does take time. However, when effective training occurs, long-term results can be beneficial to the school and community. When conflict resolution programs are infused throughout the entire school, the effects appear to be more widespread. When this occurs, the student body and faculty/staff as a whole become active problem solvers.

HOW DO I BEGIN TO IMPLEMENT ONE OF THE APPROACHES TO RESOLVING CONFLICT?

1. Setting the tone:

- Teachers can reduce conflict by helping children learn effective interactional skills, such as how to cooperate, share, make friends, respect differences of opinion, respect the rights and property of others, and respect those who are different from themselves.
- The emotional climate of the classroom should be one in which firm limits are set, but children feel safe, respected, and heard.
- The teacher needs to be available for on-the-spot support of children's communication and negotiation strategies so they can internalize these as habitual strategies for resolving conflicts.
- Schedules and routines should provide for large blocks of time for children to work together on projects. Group activities enhance the ideas of cooperation and collaboration.
- The physical environment should accommodate small-group interactions to encourage more complex social interactions. Certain children's literature books can serve as springboards for activities that help children learn social skills while cooperative grouping activities promote awareness of and respect for others' opinions.

2. Implementation:

To work effectively, specific steps and strategies should be used. Students need to acquire the skills of listening, analytical reasoning, empathizing, and be able to understand the point of view of another person. The parties with the problem need to:

- Agree that there is a problem and agree to meet.
- Identify the problem.
- Suggest possible solutions.
- Agree to one workable option.
- Finally, reach some agreement.

The students with the conflict should understand the following components: (a) an understanding of the problem or conflict; (b) some basic principles (see below); (c) some process steps that are repeated and learned to be habitual; and (d) skills learned that should become automatic responses to replace aggressive or passive behaviors (Bodine and Crawford, 1998).

Four principles of conflict resolution suggest that:

- First, those students who are ready to resolve the problem must separate the people from the problem to be able to work with others to address the issue.
- Second, the students must focus on the interests, not the positions, to satisfy the interests of each of the individuals and not take sides.
- Because the result is for all parties to gain, the third principle requires students to invent options for mutual gain. There needs to be a fair standard, impartial to both sides and one that can be applied to both sides.
- The fourth principle recommends the use of objective criteria to judge the nature of the conflict.

WHAT ARE SOME FREQUENTLY ASKED QUESTIONS ABOUT CONFLICT RESOLUTION?

1. What are some of the approaches to conflict resolution?

The four basic approaches to conflict resolution in operation in schools are: the process curriculum approach (teaching of negotiation or problem-solving skills as a distinct course each week), the mediation approach (persons are trained to mediate conflicts), the peaceable classroom approach (problem-solving skills are incorporated in the curriculum), and the peaceable school.

2. How long does it take for children to internalize conflict resolution strategies and use these on a regular basis?

Conflict resolution strategies promote children's social and emotional growth by means that help them develop self-control, self-responsibility, and self-discipline. It takes time for behavior to change. Learning takes place only through repetition and guidance from more skilled adults and peers. Once new, less aggressive habits are learned, then students can begin to help each other.

CONCLUSION

Conflicts are normal among people, but these can be solved through systematic and consistently applied conflict resolution strategies. The teacher and school can choose the strategies that best fit the needs of the children. Conflict resolution programs promote safer schools and also promote positive values like active listening, appreciating others' viewpoints, empathy, impulse control, and anger management. Benefits to the entire student body are that students often become actively involved in the problem-solving process. Conflict resolution programs provide a positive way to resolve conflicts and allow students a greater responsibility in solving their own problems.

Schools that teach students that there are positive ways to resolve conflict in the school, home, and community are promoting good citizenship and aiding in the lessening of violence in our society. Students who learn to resolve conflicts in a positive manner tend to use that same positive mind-set in their workplace and in society. As positive role models, school faculty and staff can promote cooperation and collaboration and prevent violence. The investment of time should be well considered when schools are permeated with a safe and positive atmosphere for learning and students are empowered with problem-solving skills on a daily basis.

RESOURCES

Begun, R. W. & Hunt, F. J. (Eds.). (2002). *Ready-to-Use Violence Prevention Skills: Lessons and Activities for Elementary Students.* San Francisco: Jossey Bass. This is a practical resource that includes a curriculum guide for conflict resolution for educators in K–6 classrooms. Based on real-life situations, it includes help in recognizing problems and the skills needed to resolve them.

Bodine, R. J. & Crawford, D. K. (1998). *The Handbook of Conflict Resolution Education: A Guide to Building Quality Programs in Schools.* San Francisco, CA:

Jossey-Bass, Inc. Designed to address resolving conflict at the schoolwide level, this book provides insights for classroom teachers and administrators.

Fisher, R., Ury, W., & Patton, B. (1991). *Getting to Yes: Negotiating Agreement without Giving In.* New York: Penguin. This practical book is a how-to guide to help people negotiate when resolving conflicts.

Holden, G. (1997). Changing the Way Kids Settle Conflicts. *Educational Leadership (Special Issue on Social & Emotional Learning), 54*(8): 74–76. Leaders in the field of social and emotional development as well as classroom teachers, who are leaders in their own right, present thoughtful perspectives on how to support and guide children in contemporary society.

Kostelnik, M. J., Stein, L. C., Whiren, A. P., & Soderman, A. K. (1993). *Guiding Children's Social Development* (2d ed.). New York: Delmar. While favoring and clearly identifying conflict resolution, this text also comprehensively discusses social development.

COOPERATIVE
GROUPING

I n a time when businesses expect their employees to exemplify excellent group skills on the job, cooperative grouping can begin to develop those skills during the elementary years. When cooperative grouping is implemented, students often give positive responses to the meaningful skills they obtain when solving problems, working on projects, and responding to critical issues in cooperative groups. Many respond that it is better to solve problems together as a group than to work alone.

WHAT IS MEANT BY COOPERATIVE GROUPING?

Cooperative grouping occurs when students work in small groups (or teams) of two to four on an activity, game, or project with a specific goal for a designated period of time. Cooperative grouping is a grouping strategy that lies between individualization and total class learning situations. Students, as well as teachers, usually find that they like learning better when they participate in small-group activities because they feel supported by the group and can rely on others' unique talents and knowledge.

WHAT ARE THE ADVANTAGES AND CONCERNS OF USING COOPERATIVE GROUPING?

Social skills are an essential part of learning for students in elementary school. These skills are necessary for the job market and personal relationships as well (Johnson and Johnson, 1994b). According to research reports, cooperative grouping may increase social skills and promote more positive attitudes toward subjects studied while improving student achievement (Johnson and Johnson, 1994a). Students in a cooperative grouping situation may learn to listen and respect the views of others more than in a total class situation.

There is one word of caution, however: cooperative grouping does not always run smoothly on the first attempt. At least three trial and error sessions are recommended in order to obtain a comfort level for the teacher and the students. It is also beneficial to try cooperative grouping with the class at the same time another teacher implements this type of grouping. Then the two teachers can provide support for one another while brainstorming about what works best to make cooperative grouping a positive experience for everyone. A support team of two or more teachers can enhance the discussions on how best to implement cooperative grouping situations in the classroom and which activities to use to ensure student success.

HOW SHOULD I BEGIN TO IMPLEMENT COOPERATIVE GROUPING?

First, begin with the selection of a quality activity or series of activities, which coordinate with a content unit you are currently teaching and which ensures a high rate of student success (see examples by Erickson and Goodman in the Resources section, this chapter). Next, decide on a time frame. Try cooperative grouping with pairs of students for a fifteen- to thirty-minute period two or three times per week in the beginning. Gradually increase the time and the frequency of cooperative grouping activities. Later, merge two groups of two to create groups of four. Always practice the cooperative activity yourself prior to introducing it to the class.

On the first day, select one group of four to model the rules, procedures, and the first activity itself before introducing the activity to the entire class. Be certain to allow time for questions. Your group rules (keep them simple) should be posted in a conspicuous place and easily viewed by all students (see section on rules that follows).

WHAT ARE SOME FREQUENTLY ASKED QUESTIONS ABOUT COOPERATIVE GROUPING?

1. How are groups selected?

For the initial introduction and first set of cooperative grouping activities, it is recommended that the teacher select the group members and create a heterogeneous group of four students. In creating the groups, notify the students that groups will remain intact for a given period of time such as six to nine weeks.

After the initial six weeks, random selection may be used for group formation. Students may count off by fours or be provided with color-coded geometric shapes taped to their desks to form the new groups. Yet another way to select groups is to request that students select an animal (or other) shape from a brown paper bag, held by the teacher, who immediately records it beside each name on a clipboard. This ensures random selection rather than creative group shifting by students. If students complain about a certain member of the group, the reply can be given that any group can work together for approximately six weeks knowing that at that time the groups will change.

2. What rules should be required?

Classroom rules for cooperative grouping should be clearly discussed and understood before groups begin to actively work together. All rules must be strictly enforced in order to ensure success. Rules should be few, simple, and may include such things as:

- Students are expected to work quietly. The activity is discontinued if noise rises above the acceptable noise level (see explanation below).
- If the group has a question for the teacher, each of the four group members should raise his or her hand in order to obtain the teacher's attention. (If fewer than four hands are raised, the question is not acknowledged.)
- All group members are expected to work together for the good of the group.

In addition to the rules, students should be aware of the important social skills involved in cooperative learning. Students should be encouraged to call each other by name and say encouraging words to other group members. A poster can be created of positive words or praises that students can use with each other such as: *Awesome, great idea, keep it up*. Students may also find it beneficial to create a poster of things that do not encourage and should not be used (entitled "No Put-downs"), such as: *That's not right, gross, awful, you don't get it*, and the like. A big line should be drawn through this poster to indicate "No."

3. How are group responsibilities shared?

Each group member may be assigned a specific task. Such tasks may include: (a) communicator, (b) coordinator, (c) recorder, (d) supply chief, or whatever titles the teacher and students deem appropriate (see figure 5.1). The duties of each group member are discussed first in the total class environment. Group duties should be rotated on a weekly basis and plain 5x8 cards (folded in half) that label and/or explain each task may be distributed. The duties should be numbered one through four and should rotate in numerical (and alphabetical) order.

Cooperative Grouping	Group Tasks
1 Communicator	2 Coordinator
3 Recorder	4 Supply Chief

Figure 5.1.

4. How are cooperative group activities evaluated?

Each group member evaluates his own individual work as a group member, that of other individual group members, and of the group as a whole. The use of alternative or authentic assessment is highly recommended. Informal observation (by the teacher moving around the room) will provide useful information on the skills and cooperation level of each group. The teacher, carrying a checklist on a clipboard, may check off objectives as they are met by each group. All activities do not require a letter grade. A scale of one to ten (one indicating low and ten high) can be provided for each group to provide self-evaluation on how the group felt it worked toward the selected goal.

This same scale can be taped to each group coordinator's desk and used by the teacher (on occasion) to provide a quick evaluation of how the group is progressing toward the goal. If a group should happen to be off task, a simple circling of the number two or three quickly brings them back to the task at hand.

Individual as well as group self-assessment is a beneficial part of the evaluation process. A specific activity can be evaluated for a group grade, while other activities can be divided into individual parts to provide individual grades.

5. How is control maintained?

During the practice sessions, notify the students of the acceptable noise level by asking them to introduce themselves to the persons on their left and right. After introductions are completed, state that this is an acceptable noise level for the class. Clearly and concisely inform the students that if the noise level rises above the accepted level, one warning will be given: one sharp blow on a whistle or other noisemaker. If it happens a second time and a second warning is issued, call the activity to an immediate halt and discontinue the group work for that day.

Consistency is important. When the activity is discontinued due to a high noise level, the groups will promise never to be that loud again, but the teacher must hold firm. This will be an unpopular stand. If maintained, however, it bodes well for future cooperative grouping activities and the maintenance of a manageable noise level during group activities at all times. It is imperative that students understand that the acceptable level of noise in the classroom is mandatory with no negotiation allowed.

Additional noisemakers such as a harmonica, tambourine, triangle, bongo drum, train whistle, raccoon squaller, or loon call may be substituted for the whistle. After approximately one month, substitute the harmonica for the whistle to instantly obtain student attention to the fact that the noise level is becoming too loud, hence a first warning is being issued. Changing the warning signal from time to time adds new interest and awareness of the importance of maintaining a moderate noise level to ensure positive working conditions.

CONCLUSION

Cooperative learning activities, when varied, well planned, and implemented cohesively, can add a creative touch to the classroom. Selecting quality activities that are content-oriented, training and modeling the tasks for students, and providing time for questions and feedback can enhance the grade-level curriculum.

"Carefully constructed cooperative learning ensures that students are cognitively, physically, emotionally, and psychologically actively involved in constructing their own knowledge and is an important step in changing the passive and impersonal character of many classrooms" (Johnson and Johnson, 1994a, p. 263).

Students engaging in cooperative learning activities recognize that these sessions provide mutual benefits to them as individuals and to the group as a whole. Teachers can enhance social skills and content information while implementing quality cooperative learning activities in the classroom. The formation of a teacher support group can assist in the selection of a wide variety of cooperative tasks and the implementation of new ideas. Research the activities well and keep adding exceptional cooperative learning activities and strategies to your collection.

RESOURCES

Ellis, S. S. & Whalen, S. F. (1990). *Cooperative Learning: Getting Started.* New York: Scholastic. A user-friendly book on the whys and wherefores of implementing cooperative grouping

Erickson, T. (1996). *United We Solve.* Oakland, CA: Eeps Media. This latest version of cooperative grouping activities illustrates quality selections for upper elementary and middle school students.

Erickson, T. (1989). *Get It Together.* Berkeley, CA: EQUALS, Lawrence Hall of Science. Erickson's first book includes clues for cooperative group activities in the areas of mathematics, science, and social studies.

Gibbs, J. (2000). *Tribes: A New Way of Learning and Being Together.* Sausalito, CA: CenterSource Systems. This writer provides background information and activities that can lead to successful implementation of cooperative activities in the classroom. It provides ideas for parent and administration involvement and strategies to use in diverse classrooms.

Goodman, J. (1992). *Group Solutions: Cooperative Logic Activities.* Berkeley, CA: GEMS, Lawrence Hall of Science. Providing a variety of cooperative grouping activities, this book is designed for use with primary students.

Johnson, D. W. & Johnson, R. (1994a). *Learning Together and Alone: Cooperative, Competitive, and Individualistic Learning.* Boston: Allyn and Bacon. This classic work by Johnson and Johnson is a must for any professional library.

Johnson, D. W. & Johnson, R. (1994b). *The New Circles of Learning: Cooperation in the Classroom and School.* Alexandria, VA: Association for Supervision and Curriculum Development. This updated book on the advantages of implementing cooperative learning in the classroom is teacher friendly in its approach and includes a research background.

Kagan, S. (1994). *Cooperative Learning.* San Clemente, CA: Kagan. Kagan provides background research on cooperative learning and its strategies. Planning and assessment ideas are an integral part of this book.

Seymour, D. (1982). *Favorite Problems.* Palo Alto, CA: Dale Seymour. This popular publication provides an outstanding selection of quality problem situations for use in small cooperative groups.

Thousand, J. S., Villa, R. A., & Nevin, A. I. (Eds.). (2000). *Creativity and Collaborative Learning.* Baltimore, MD: Paul H. Brookes. This collection of articles on cooperative learning and collaboration would be an important contribution to any library. It is a practical guide to empower students, families, and teachers.

6

CRITICAL
AND CREATIVE
THINKING SKILLS

During their study of the 1886 Gold Rush, a team of four children are hovering around the computer at their workstation. Print-outs of the team's thinking strategies used the previous day are posted in plain view. The teacher asks, "What did those who found gold do with their money? Determine which 'miner' stories are valid and which were fabricated." The children's Internet search revealed how some squandered their money, but also a man named Fair, in San Francisco, started building a now-famous hotel.

The students then weigh the positive and negative impacts of instant wealth and then type these into a graphic organizer they created on the computer. The teacher interjects, "Hum, is it possible that Leila and Brad are contradicting each other?" They weigh the alternatives. Then, before students engage in discussions to consider what having a lot of money might mean today, they refer to the "procedural checklist for decision making" to scaffold the process. These students are using creative thinking when looking at the situation from multiple perspectives and are using critical thinking to make informed judgements.

WHAT IS MEANT BY CRITICAL AND
CREATIVE THINKING SKILLS?

Critical thinking, one of the subskills of functional thinking, involves making reasoned judgements. It is a process of analyzing a problem by examining the facts, acting on these with logic and arriving at plausible conclusions. The purpose of critical thinking is to determine authenticity based on a determined criteria, or to determine the reasonable nature of decisions. We are engaged in critical thinking in our personal, social, and political lives, when we, for example, write a book review or respond to an editorial, if we go beyond initial interpretations or feelings. Critical thinking requires weighing the information and the reliability of the sources before forming conclusions. This process requires the use of inductive thinking—drawing inferential conclusions on the basis of repeated observations that yielded promising but incomplete data—and it requires deductive thinking—drawing a logical conclusion in which the premises were related and supported the argument.

Creative thinking is important to critical thinking in terms of exploring potential solutions. Creativity involves taking objects or thoughts and recreating these in novel ways for new purposes. Cognitive dimensions of creative thinking require fluency (being able to generate multiple responses), flexibility (approaching ideas and situations beyond the obvious), originality (combining ideas to make a new one or producing novel ideas), and elaboration (expanding on ideas or details). Becoming a creative or a critical thinker requires outside forces (such as selected teaching strategies) that motivate, impact, or support a person's internal talents. Further qualities of creative and critical thinkers are their willingness to take risks and use their imaginations.

WHAT ARE THE ADVANTAGES AND CONCERNS OF DECISIONS TO USE SELECTED SUBSKILLS OF FUNCTIONAL THINKING?

Critical thinking is one type of thinking humans use to process information; each type has unique and sometimes complimentary purposes and processes. Beyer (1997) organizes thinking types according to function, but all may be enacted simultaneously or in various combinations. Recalling and recording information are central to the perception and organization of information. Reasoning and processing are used to generate meaning.

When an unusual outcome or improvement is needed, creative thinking is employed, and when reasonable judgement is needed—a critical thinking process is utilized. Decision making, problem solving, and conceptualizing are used when we encounter an obstacle or must choose among alternatives. Assessing, planning, and monitoring provide planning information for the next step or needed reteaching. The opportunity to look back and learn from the thinking process—metacognition—provides the feedback to learn new thinking strategies.

HOW DO I BEGIN TO PROVIDE AN ENVIRONMENT THAT STIMULATES CRITICAL AND CREATIVE THINKING?

- Provide a learning environment that fosters possibilities for thinking and supports student thinking. Productive learning tasks centered around thoughtful questions provide repeated opportunities for students to engage in thinking and to sustain thinking. To encourage thinking, negative risks, such as humiliation for response, must be eliminated. Students must be given wait time after questions are asked. Teachers should model the behaviors and dispositions of careful thought.
- Make visible and explicit the thinking steps or elements that are needed for quality thinking and productive outcomes. Help students see the steps they take (metacognition) in the thinking process and then help them compare and contrast these with the steps "experts" take when solving a problem. Students' responses should be documented and displayed to highlight successes, but also to guide future discussions.
- Scaffold and support student thinking through cues, questions, graphic organizers, and procedural checklists of suggested mental steps to use for a specific thinking procedure. Help students rehearse the steps by having peers suggest routines or procedures that can be employed.
- Integrate thinking instruction in the context of learning real-subject matter, not as an isolated skill. National Standards for each of the content areas requires some type of thinking and reasoning. Decisions about the kind of thinking needed and the direction for the thinking process is affected by the subject matter learned. Learning thinking skills while learning important content such as math or social studies also makes the

learning of both content and thought process skill more meaningful. What is formed is a "connected building block" to attach later learning.

WHAT ARE SOME FREQUENTLY ASKED QUESTIONS ABOUT CRITICAL THINKING?

1. What are the essential elements of critical thinking?

Critical thinking requires simultaneous interaction of the following six elements:

- Dispositions are habitual ways of thinking, such as skepticism. This requires questioning the authenticity, accuracy, and plausibility. Reasons must support assertions. Fair-mindedness and different points of view are valued. Perseverance and integrity prevail.
- Criteria such as values, standards, definitions, requirements, rules, and/or test results must be applied to make judgements. Judgements include: determining relevance, verifying facts, determining the credibility of the source of written/verbal information or observation, identifying ambiguous claims, detecting bias, identifying logical fallacies, identifying logical inconsistencies, and determining the strength of an argument.
- Argument refers to a proposition with supporting evidence (facts) and reasoning that is used to convince. To be strong, an argument must have a clear position/claim, convincing reasons for the claim, including reasons why counter claims are invalid, relevant facts, conditions that may limit the claim, and a logical order of premises that lead conclusively to the claim.
- Reasoning is process used to infer from facts and assumptions. Determining the strength of a conclusion requires examination of the line of reasoning and the logical relationships.
- Point of view is the position from which one makes meaning. Because it is formed from prior experience, culture, values, and self-expectations, it shapes what each chooses to observe. To more accurately and fairly make decisions, critical thinkers examine several others' points of view as well as their own.

• Procedures for applying criteria to think critically requires a number of procedures and levels of questioning to establish meaning and accuracy. Socratic questioning is used during the process to probe beyond superficial thinking; to: seek reasons and evidence; look for implications and consequences; distinguish what is known from what is believed; and detect inconsistencies, overgeneralizations, and vagueness. To scaffold students through the process, teachers can provide specific procedural lists— steps to take under the following circumstances: (a) before coming to a conclusion; (b) when judging the credibility of a source (i.e., news editorial); or (c) when determining the strength of an argument.

2. How are critical and creative thinking related to decision making?

Some processes, such as making a good decision, require several types of thinking, such as: (a) defining the problem; (b) identifying the criteria of the "best" decision; (c) identifying alternatives; (d) predicting likely consequences and cost of each alternative; (e) evaluating the presumed consequences of each alternative in terms of the criteria of the "best" choice; and (f) selecting the alternative that most nearly approximates the criteria of the "best" choice. The second and the fifth steps involve critical thinking, while the third step requires creative thinking. Knowing when to employ critical thinking requires careful consideration of the elements used during the thinking process.

CONCLUSION

Even for students who had been poor-performing, if their teachers attend to the cognitive skills needed to understand the content to be learned, students will attain higher subject-matter achievement.

RESOURCES

Beyer, B. K. (1997). *Improving Student Thinking: A Comprehensive Approach.* Needham, MA: Allyn and Bacon. How and why children and adults utilize selected subskills of functional thinking to process and use information is illustrated in this book.

Garmston, R. & Wellman, B. (1998). Teacher Talk That Makes a Difference. *Educational Leadership, 55*(7): 30–35. Essential to critical thinking is how teachers scaffold children's emerging ideas as well as foster skills for thinking, the main issue in this article.

Hannel, G. I. & Hannel, L. (1998). 7 Steps to Teach Critical Thinking. *Education Digest, 64*(1): 47–52. As the title states, this digest provides practical steps for teachers to consider when developing a curriculum that supports critical thinking.

Honig, A. S. (2000). Promoting Creativity in Young Children. (ED442548). ERIC document available through www.edrs.com. This book explains creativity in young children and provides strategies, such as bibliotherapy for developing divergent thinking and supporting social and emotional development through creative activities.

Isenberg, J. P. & Jalongo, M. R. (2001). *Creative Expression and Play in Early Childhood.* Upper Saddle River, NJ: Merrill Prentice Hall.

Lynch, M. D. & Harris, C. R. (Eds.). (2001). *Fostering Creativity in Children, K–8: Theory and Practice.* Needham, MA: Allyn & Bacon. This book provides general strategies for developing creativity, special strategies for each of the content areas, and attention to creativity for special populations.

Marzano, R. J. (1998). What Are the General Skills of Thinking and Reasoning and How Do You Teach Them? *Clearing House, 71*(5): 268–74. National Standards thinking skills are examined in light of teaching strategies researched to be effective pathways for children to achieve those standards.

Rosenshine, B. V. & Meister, C. (1992). The Use of Scaffolds for Teaching Higher Order Cognitive Strategies. *Educational Leadership, 49*(April): 26–33. Rather than direct instruction, learning to use critical thinking is a process that requires expert scaffolding from teachers and more knowledgeable peers.

Savage, L. B. (1998). Eliciting Critical Thinking Skills through Questioning. *Clearing House, 71*(5): 291–94. Knowing the right questions to ask at the right time is one of ways to scaffold the critical thinking processes children can learn to use.

Websites

The Creativity Web: www.ozemail.com.au/~caveman/Creative. The Creativity Web is by Charles Cave in Sydney, Australia, with books, software, people, organizations, quotations, techniques, the brain, and much more!

Enchanted Mind: www.enchantedmind.com. This site has a great deal of information on creativity techniques and inspiring articles, as well as puzzles, including some interactive Java puzzles.

Brain Dancing: www.bdance.com. A fascinating website by Patrick McGee and complementary to his book of the same title.

Multimedia magazine: www.volusia.com/creative. A multimedia magazine on creativity, innovation, and change produced by Adventures in Creativity, Inc.

Mind Tools: www.mindtools.com. Mind Tools—techniques for memory, creativity, and skills for high-performance living and practical psychology; shareware programs are available.

Odyssey of the Mind: www.odysseyofthemind.org. Odyssey of the Mind—promoting creative team-based problem solving in a school program for students from kindergarten through college.

7

FAMILY INVOLVEMENT

Keisha and her mom get ready quickly because the van is coming to take them to the computer workshop at school. That night, a volunteer instructor from the local hospital taught database management that Keisha used in her social studies class. The school, with community support, had several hands-on workshops for families to learn skills that their children use in class. Families then had more understanding to be able to actively participate in their children's schoolwork. Keisha and her mom are experiencing some of the supports realized as important for the single-parent involvement to make her child's schooling successful. But family involvement in schools has not always taken this same form.

WHAT IS MEANT BY FAMILY INVOLVEMENT AND PARTNERSHIP WITH TEACHERS?

Parents' participation in their children's schooling has been impacted by changes in family and society structures. From the 1880s to 1900, schooling in America was a community-based effort for many rural and small town families who needed their children to tend the farms during the growing seasons but desired their children to grow up reading, writing, and doing basic mathematics. Common were one-room schoolhouses with all children learning together with a teacher who was hired, paid, and sometimes housed by families. Families had considerable voice in school matters. By the1950s, family life shifted to a more modern industrial society with a majority of fathers working outside the home and mothers staying home to raise the family. The roles for parents' involvement in their child's education were helping and supporting teachers by joining the Parent Teacher Association (PTA), helping with homework, helping with fund-raisers, and coming to school at specified times for conferences and back-to-school nights. Schools were and still are run by local governments and school boards and families began to experience a more distant relationship in governing decisions.

In the last fifty years, considerable changes in the family structure and increased cultural pluralism has shifted the ways families can or desire to participate in their children's schooling. There are more single-parent families or both parents working outside of the home and increasingly diverse cultural values and customs represented by families in schools. While family structures have shifted, contemporary research indicates strong family roles in schooling are still needed to ensure student academic achievement. A school environment that provides children opportunities they would not experience at home but also allows children the comfort needed to make sense of the world by partnering with families affords the greatest chances for student success (Zellman & Waterman, 1998). Ideally, a combination of support by society's institutions, such as home, school, physicians, and friends, would contribute to the uninterrupted and logical flow between children's home life and schoolwork, such as the family night Keisha and her mom (earlier) experienced.

Successful family-school relationships are those that view families as partners in children's education. "Family friendly" schools:

1. invite families to visit and make the building a cheerful, welcoming place;
2. meet families on their own turf and teachers sometimes make home visits;
3. make it easy for families to find out what is going on in school;
4. inform families when their children are doing well;
5. respect and accommodate families, culture, language, and desired type of involvement; talk to parents in plain language and not in education jargon;

6. involve families in the school's decision-making process; and

7. hold meaningful, problem-solving, and hands-on meetings at times convenient for families.

WHAT ARE SOME ADVANTAGES AND CHALLENGES TO FORMING PARTNERSHIPS BETWEEN FAMILIES AND SCHOOLS?

Parenting is a difficult task that schools and teachers can support. Some parents lack valuable skills that school faculty, many of whom are parents themselves, can share. Parents may not realize the great job they are doing raising their child. School recognition of their dedication can boost a family's self-esteem.

Not only do families need feedback, but so too do teachers need praise from families to help them feel competent about their professional roles. Teachers also benefit when they have open communication with families as that information can be valuable for effective teaching of the wide range of learners in their classes. Inviting families in to share complementing expertise during instructional time widens the life experiences for all children in the class.

While research studies confirm a relationship between parent involvement and children's academic improvement as reported by improved test scores, the following presents why families are either involved with or stay away from school. A parent's enthusiasm (the extent to which parenting is rewarding) and a positive parenting style have been found to relate higher in children's school success than even parents' direct involvement in school through such avenues as, for example, a parent volunteering during the school day. Both parental enthusiasm and direct involvement in school functions, though, may be motivators for parental involvement in their child's school improvement (Berger, 1999).

Schools may enhance these motivators by providing parenting workshops or by connecting families with needed social services. Having a greater understanding of the roles of parenting through workshops, especially for young families, single families, and those with no relatives nearby, can improve families' feelings of being supported and hence improve support of their children in school and at home. Providing pathways to social services to help families acquire basic daily needs can reduce day-to-day stresses that might supersede family's efforts for their child's schooling. Schools that provide for family's as well as individual children's basic needs can improve the overall qualities surrounding learning for families and schools to work together to help children succeed.

Other factors that challenge successful family-school partnerships involve role confusion or a lack of understanding of the other's point of view. Some families may feel it is the school's sole responsibility for their child's academic success. Some teachers may feel that they are the "experts" on academic achievement and parents should have no say in curriculum decisions.

The school administration and teachers' lack of understanding of families' points of view based on their cultures and how certain families interrelate can also impede those children's academic success. Schools might need to look for nontraditional strategies for relating to families from minority, low-income, or culturally diverse backgrounds. The traditional style of public schools is analytical and individual oriented, while many minority families favor a relational style. Rather than listening to a lecture or working alone on tasks, some families may enjoy hands-on activities and working in groups, with ample opportunities for stimulating dialogue. Some families who learn through a more hands-on approach would be turned off to school functions if teachers and administrators hold workshops or open houses that only talk at them (Barbour & Barbour, 2000; Hampton & Mumford, 1998).

While all families want their child to get a good education, some adults who did not experience academic successes as children may not participate in school functions or appear resistant to partnerships because school, as they experienced it, was not a friendly place for them. Teachers and administrators can share the responsibility to make the school a welcoming place by approaching families through strategies they enjoy, providing information in plain language and in their native language, and by involving them directly in school decision making.

HOW DO I BEGIN TO DEVELOP PARTNERSHIPS WITH FAMILIES?

Before you begin either a schoolwide (preferred) or one-teacher-in-one-class improvement of family-school partnerships, first consider your own beliefs and current practices regarding families and their role in schooling.

1. Consider your beliefs about the role of the principal in school-family partnerships.
2. How do you view family participation in schooling—volunteering in the classroom, going on field trips, joining in curriculum planning?
3. What kinds of staff development would you find helpful for learning effective parent involvement strategies?
4. How much do you know about the culture traditions of the children in your class?

Examine home-school partnership practices that currently exist or you would like to exist.

1. What strategies are you using with families of children in your own class?
2. Which families are hardest to reach?
3. What are other teachers in your school doing? What does the principal do?
4. How active is the PTA in your school and what functions does it have?
5. What practices does your school have and what should change to be more effective? What improvements would you make?
6. What costs and personnel are involved with the costs you propose?

Start by examining how you want your school-family partnership practices to look in three years. Consider the steps it would take to get there. Start first with one strategy you feel would be most successful; for example, develop a system for regularly calling homes when students are excelling or improving in academics. Then build on your successes (Gestwicki, 1999).

WHAT ARE SOME FREQUENTLY ASKED QUESTIONS ABOUT FAMILY INVOLVEMENT?

1. What are some basic types of parent involvement?

Joyce Epstein, at the Johns Hopkins University Center on Families, Communities, Schools, and Children's Learning, describes six types of parental involvement. See http://scov.csos.jhu.edu/p2000/center.htm.

- Parenting: While respecting each family's culture, strengths, and efforts, the school provides resources or positive parenting workshops to assist families to create home environments that support children's overall well-being.
- Communicating: Considering the unique language and parenting styles, the school designs more effective forms of home-school and school-home communications to increase families' understanding of school policies.
- Volunteering: To reap the benefits of families' talents and to help families understand the role of the teacher, schools set up a range of opportunities for parents to volunteer (i.e., reading with young children during school or organizing a telephone calling tree, outside of school hours).
- Learning at Home: To help students gain positive attitudes about homework and to assist families to gain the confidence to help their children, schools provide multiple types of opportunities for families to learn how to help their children at home with homework and other curricular activities.
- Decision Making: Family representation in school decisions that links all families with parent representation provides families a feeling of ownership in the school.
- Collaborating with the Community: Resources and services from the community are linked with school academic and social goals to strengthen students' achievement.

2. How Should Families of Children with Special Needs Be Involved?

For children with special needs, the new reauthorization of IDEA (special education law) in 1997 clearly describes the importance of family involvement in the child's educational placements. Rather than viewing children and their families at risk, the construct "children and families at promise" conveys the potential all children hold and the gift that each family can contribute.

CONCLUSION

Dorothy Rich, founder and president of the Home and School Institute in Washington, DC (http://www.megaskillshsi.org), recommends teachers learn the three R's of working with families : (a) Reassurance that the school is meeting their child's needs; (b) Recognition of the critical role families play in their children's academic lives, but teachers also see themselves in key roles in that success; and (c) Respect for the responsibility families have.

RESOURCES

Barbour, C. & Barbour, N. H. (2000). *Families, Schools, and Communities: Building Partnerships for Educating Children* (2d ed.). Upper Saddle River, NJ: Pearson Education, Inc. With a culturally sensitive approach to education, the book provides both classroom climate suggestions and strategies for involving communities and families as partners in their children's education.

Berger, E. H. (1999). *Parents As Partners in Education: The School and Home Working Together* (5th ed.). Upper Saddle River, NJ: Pearson Education, Inc. A popular text that provides a wide range of strategies that are explained in light of existing research on effective partnerships.

Boult, B. & Walberg, H. J. (1999). *176 Ways to Involve Parents.* Glenview, IL: Skylight Professional Development. Realistic and ready-to-use ideas for working with families in this book help families to feel welcome, to develop ongoing communication, and to become involved in governance.

Gestwicki, C. (1999). *Home, School, and Community Relations: A Guide to Working with Parents* (4th ed.). Albany, NY: Delmar. Suggestions for early childhood educators are included in this book to provide practical solutions for families and schools to work closely together.

Hampton, F. M. & Mumford, D. A. (1998). Parent Involvement in Inner-City Schools: The Project FAST Extended Family Approach to Success. *Urban Education, 33*(3): 410–28. Teachers are given opportunities to understand and capitalize on extended family style of support children from inner-city schools receive.

Pape, B. (1999). Involving Parents Lets Students and Teachers Win. *Education Digest, 64*(6): 47–53. This concise digest illustrates some of the advantages of involving families in their children's schooling.

Zellman, G. L. & Waterman, J. M. (1998). Understanding the Impact of Parent School Involvement on Children's Educational Outcomes. *Journal of Educational Research, 91*(6): 370–81. Research provides implications for the types of ways families support their children's successes.

CONTACTS (http://www.ncrel.org/sdrs/areas/issues/envrnmnt/
famncomm/pa100.htm)

Center on School, Family, and Community Partnerships
(formerly Center on Families, Communities, Schools, and Children's Learning)
Johns Hopkins University
3505 N. Charles St.
Baltimore, MD 21218
(410) 516-8800; fax (410) 516-8890
Contact: Joyce Epstein, Director
E-mail: Jepstein@inet.ws.gov
http://scov.csos.jhu.edu/p2000/center.htm

Home and School Institute
MegaSkills Education Center
1500 Massachusetts Ave., N.W.
Washington, DC 20005
(202) 466-3633; fax (202) 833-1400
Contact: Sandra Getner, Outreach Coordinator
http://www.megaskillshsi.org

Institute for Responsive Education
605 Commonwealth Ave.
Boston, MA 02215
(617) 353-3309; fax (617) 353-8444
Contact: Scott Thompson, Director of Dissemination and Project Development
E-mail: stt@bu.edu
http://www.resp-ed.org/

National Coalition for Parent Involvement in Education
Box 39, 1201 16th St., N.W.
Washington, DC 20036
(202) 822-8405 ext. 53; fax (202) 872-4050
Contact: Sue Ferguson
E-mail: FERGUSON@IEL.ORG

National Parent Information Network
ERIC Clearinghouse on Elementary and Early Childhood Education

University of Illinois
805 W. Pennsylvania Ave.
Urbana, IL 61801-4897
(217) 333-3767 (800) 583-4135; fax 217-333-3767
Contact: Anne R. Robertson/Research Associate
E-mail: ericeece@uiuc.educ.edu
http://npin.org/
Parents as Teachers National Center
10176 Corporate Square Drive, Suite 230
St. Louis, MO 63132
(314) 432-4330; fax (314) 432-8963
Contact: Rand Myles, Network System Administrator
E-mail: patnc@patnc.org/
http://www.patnc.org/
Partnership for Family Involvement in Education
(formerly Family Involvement Partnership for Learning)
600 Independence Ave., S.W.
Washington, DC 20202-8173
(800) USA-LEARN or (202) 401-0091; fax (202) 205-9133
E-mail: Partner@ed.gov
http://pfie.ed.gov/

HANDS-ON DISCOVERY SCIENCE LEARNING

R esearch tells us that learning is more meaningful when it is experienced rather than merely explained. Teachers are now encouraged to be facilitators of learning rather than chief dispensers of knowledge. The old Chinese Proverb summarizes this clearly: "I hear and I forget. I see and I remember. I do and I understand."

WHAT IS MEANT BY HANDS-ON DISCOVERY SCIENCE LEARNING?

Teachers and scientists generally agree that one of the best ways to teach science is through an active approach that encourages all students to interact with the world around them by utilizing the science process skills of observation, measurement, prediction, inference, communication, and experimentation. A hands-on discovery learning approach in science follows Piaget's theories concerning the importance of considering students' interests and learning styles when designing activities. Other names for this approach are a problem-solving approach, inquiry-based learning, problem-centered teaching, and investigations. As soon as the problem is posed, prior knowledge is determined, questions determine what information should be gathered, tentative solutions are suggested, research is conducted, and results are analyzed to draw conclusions.

This approach is consistent with the constructivist learning theories in which students actively construct learning based on their prior knowledge. Constructivists stress that students must develop their own ideas rather than have the ideas presented to them in a lecture format. The meaningful development of knowledge can then be used to make sense of the surrounding world. Problems are also posed that enable students to find answers that are relevant to their lives. To this extent, students are actually handling and experiencing science in order to learn science.

WHAT ARE THE ADVANTAGES AND CONCERNS ABOUT IMPLEMENTING HANDS-ON DISCOVERY SCIENCE LEARNING?

Hands-on discovery science learning stimulates students' divergent thinking and their natural curiosity about the world. In order to move away from the perception of science as the memorization of facts and formulas, students become scientists performing experiments and examining the results to generate meaning. The teacher's responsibility is to create situations that latch on to students' curiosities and enable meaningful science investigations to occur on a regular basis, both in and out of the elementary classroom. The goal of education is the acquisition of knowledge. The aim of discovery science learning, however, is to construct knowledge acquired through time rather than knowledge that is learned passively. Knowledge built on self-discovery tends to be more valued by students in the long run.

When mentioning concerns, some teachers state that this type of learning takes more time and preparation. If you start small and acquire discovery learning activities and lessons over time, it is not difficult to implement. Being part of a support team of teachers enables activities/units to be shared and saves time in the long run.

Another concern is that discovery learning is implemented in an open atmosphere where student conversations and discussions about the activity may lead to a higher noise level. If the accepted noise level is discussed and implemented (see chapter 5), quality work can be accomplished in such an atmosphere. In many cases, students may be more verbal, but every student in the class is on task and highly engaged in the learning process.

HOW SHOULD I BEGIN TO IMPLEMENT DISCOVERY SCIENCE LEARNING?

A unit on Air and Air Pressure might serve as an example of one way to implement discovery science learning into the curriculum. The teacher begins by asking, "What is air?" Students might conclude that:

- Air is all around us.
- It takes up space.
- It is real. Or
- Air provides pressure.

The teacher then may ask, "What are some of the properties of air?" and "How could we find out about these properties?" Using the experiments in Carin and Bass's book *Teaching Science As Inquiry* (2001, pp. A 48–49) the teacher chooses a specific experiment such as "What Is Air?" Students begin by defining how they know that air is real by swinging first their hands and then a piece of paper through space in order to feel the air. Students observe, infer, and hypothesize about the nature of air and record their results.

The teacher then asks students to hypothesize what will happen when they place a glass upside down straight into a bowl or dishpan of water (colored with green food coloring). Students write their hypotheses in their journals. Next, they perform the action and discuss the results. Once again, students record this information and their reflections on what they learned.

Then the teacher asks, "What might happen if we tilt the glass prior to placing it in the water? Will the results be the same once again?" Students make a hypothesis and record it. She then turns the glass sideways and places it in the water. Students note and record their results. Class discussion follows. There are numerous quality hands-on activities that demonstrate the properties of air (see Resources, this chapter).

In order to engage the students, high-level questions are asked, such as:

- What caused this to happen?
- How could you change the experiment?
- What would happen if you placed two glasses in the water?

- Based on what you now know, how would you explain this experiment to a younger student?
- Why do you think this is an important experiment to observe?
- What conclusions can you draw?
- How could you create a similar experiment to explain the same property using different objects?

WHAT ARE SOME FREQUENTLY ASKED QUESTIONS ABOUT HANDS-ON DISCOVERY LEARNING?

1. What are these science process skills and why are they important in hands-on discovery learning?

The science process skills (often listed with varying names and definitions) are those skills that enable the student to understand and apply knowledge about the universe. Hands-on discovery science lessons should include the use of science process skills in order to promote meaningful learning. The names and brief descriptions of the science process skills follow.

- Observing: using all of the senses to gather information.
- Classifying: placing basic items into like groups with common features.
- Predicting: making a guess based on a minimal amount of information.
- Measuring: gathering accurate and specific data.
- Inferring: making a conjecture based on minimal data.
- Experimenting: constructing and completing the experiment while controlling the variables, manipulating the data, and assessing the results.
- Communicating: disseminating information in an organized manner.

Hands-on discovery science learning is *not* confined to one particular class period per day or week. It is *not* reading a chapter in a textbook and answering questions in order to prepare for the Friday test. It is *not* performing a science experiment or demonstration for fun without forming a hypothesis, discussing prior knowledge, implementing content knowledge, using the science process skills, and concluding with a reflection. Hands-on discovery *is* relevant to students' lives because a problem is posed and students then work through the science process skills to discover a solution on their own.

2. What are the *National Science Education Standards* and how do they relate to hands-on discovery learning?

The *National Science Education Standards* (1996) were designed to offer guidelines for teachers, curriculum developers, teacher educators, and school districts. The Standards promote the idea that the acquisition of science knowledge and understanding should be a central focus of all education. They demonstrate the importance of science literacy in today's world. The Standards emphasize understanding (more than memorizing facts), integrating all science content, and covering fewer topics, but adding more depth to those few (see chapter 17). Some of the major themes of the Standards are:

- Science is learned by doing science (quality science experiences).
- Science is learned by inquiry (understanding how scientists think).
- Science is learned by collaborating (working together in groups).
- Science is learned over a period of time (time to digest, understand, and reflect).
- Science is learned by developing personal knowledge (constructing meaningful understanding).

"Full inquiry involves students asking a simple question, completing an investigation, answering the question, and presenting the results to others. Student questions might arise from previous investigations, planned classroom activities, or questions students ask each other" (National Research Council, 1996, pp. 121–22).

CONCLUSION

To make science meaningful, students should be engaged in hands-on learning, be able to propose solutions, complete research, and take action. The teacher, as facilitator, observes, listens, and asks high-level questions while implementing the use of the science process skills and standards in order to promote the meaningful development of science knowledge within the classroom. "Science in the elementary classroom can be more usefully seen as an adventure to be experienced than as a collection of concepts to be passively acquired. Science education reform movements encourage the development of habits of mind to emphasize this process" (Tippins, Koballa, and Payne, 2002, p. 196).

RESOURCES

Carin, A. A. & Bass, J. E. (2001). *Teaching Science As Inquiry.* Upper Saddle River, NJ: Merrill Prentice Hall. Good practices and practical suggestions are provided here with quality science experiments that can be easily implemented.

Fredericks, A. D. & Cheesebrough, D. L. (1993). *Science for All Children.* New York: HarperCollins. Excellent chapters including questioning skills and authentic assessment in this book provide quality implementation ideas for the elementary teacher.

Good, T. L. & Brophy, J. E. (2003). *Looking in Classrooms.* New York: Addison Wesley (Pearson). This is a teacher-friendly book that includes chapters on the benefits of meaningful hands-on learning. Chapters 9 and 10 are of particular interest for science implementation.

Koch, J. (1999). *Science Stories: Teachers and Children as Science Learners.* Boston: Houghton Mifflin. From questioning skills to technology in the classroom, this writer includes many useful chapters on "doing science."

National Research Council. (1996). *National Science Education Standards.* Washington, DC: National Academy Press. Knowledge of the National Science Standards will greatly enhance understanding of the ways and means to improve science learning and teaching in the classroom.

Tippins, D. J., Koballa Jr., T. R., & Payne, B. D. (2002). *Learning from Cases: Unraveling The Complexities of Elementary Science Teaching.* Boston: Allyn and Bacon. This resource encourages the implementation of science reform emphasizing the process approach.

9

INCLUSION OF
CHILDREN WITH
SPECIAL NEEDS

Inclusion of children with special needs in settings with their typically developing peers is not an option; it is the law. Public Law 94-142, most recently reauthorized in 1997 as the Individuals with Disabilities Act (IDEA), entitles children with diagnosed disabilities, ages three to twenty-one a "free and public education," but also requires every child with a disability be educated in the least restrictive environment (see chapter 2).

WHAT IS MEANT BY INCLUSION?

IDEA states that children with special needs are to be given access to the same or similar educational experiences as their peers who are typically developing. To the fullest amount possible, schools need to provide children with disabilities the opportunity to be included in classrooms with their peers who are typically developing, supporting the belief and ethics that the needs and interests of children with special needs are more like their typically developing peers than they are different.

WHAT ARE THE ADVANTAGES AND CONCERNS REGARDING THE INCLUSION OF CHILDREN WITH SPECIAL NEEDS IN CLASSROOMS WITH THEIR TYPICALLY DEVELOPING PEERS (GENERAL EDUCATION CLASSROOMS)?

Classroom research supports inclusion for ALL children for several reasons. Quality inclusive programming benefits children with special needs, but also children who are typically developing.

Children with special needs:

1. have opportunities to observe, imitate, and interact with typically developing peers who have acquired higher levels of social, cognitive, or motor abilities;
2. can learn more easily from typically developing peers who may more readily communicate at their levels than the teacher can; and
3. may be more motivated to try a little harder when surrounded by typically developing peers than if surrounded by only other children with special needs.

Children who are typically developing benefit from inclusion:

1. when they tutor a child with special needs because they have to more fully learn a task or information to be able to explain it clearly; hence typically developing children increase their own skills and understandings; and
2. because they can develop greater awareness and sensitivity to the diversity of people.

There are some challenges to including children with disabilities in general education classrooms, too. Special education and general education teachers, as well as families:

1. may have initial anxiety that the children with special needs will not be adequately served because they believe that general education teachers do not have the necessary skills. In fact, general education teachers

will need some specialized preparation to differentiate the curriculum and assessment for diverse learners;

2. may be concerned that typically developing children will not receive needed attention, because the teacher would have to spend more time with the children with special needs. Quality programs with teachers who have some specialized preparation and models in which special education and general education teachers collaboratively teach have been found to appropriately meet the needs of both children with and without special needs; and

3. may wonder if typically developing children will imitate immature or inappropriate behaviors of children with special needs, yet the research suggests this does not happen.

HOW DO I BEGIN TO INCLUDE CHILDREN WITH SPECIAL NEEDS IN CLASSES WITH THEIR TYPICALLY DEVELOPING PEERS?

The experience and level of inclusion varies for every child and for every family. Appropriate programs for ALL children should be challenging, yet provide the kinds of supports any child may need. In an inclusive classroom ALL students should feel that: (a) they are respected members of the group, (b) they are given the kinds of teacher guidance needed to help them interact successfully with their peers, and (c) the classroom routines and academic tasks are geared to support their learning styles and abilities. The educational programming goal is to plan a program match with the family's and the child's needs and interests.

- Successful inclusion requires planning, teamwork, and support. Teachers, families, and, as needed, occupational therapists, social workers, physical therapists, speech therapists, and physicians will need extra time for planning in their efforts to work together to provide appropriate services for children with special needs in the general education classroom.
- This collaborative planning and monitoring of each child's Individual Education Plan (IEP) should guide the child's experiences.

- For some children with special needs, spending only part of their day in general education classrooms is the most appropriate and least restrictive environment.
- Other children, with supports from specialists and curriculum modifications, will be fully included all day with their peers who are typically developing.

WHAT ARE SOME FREQUENTLY ASKED QUESTIONS ABOUT INCLUSION?

1. What are some effective teaching models?

Coteaching between a general education teacher and a special education teacher is a practice that has shown great success. Models for coteaching range from direct, in which two or more teachers directly serve [students] together, to more indirect, in which teachers plan together or share ideas before or after school. One desired practice is for the special education teacher to come into the general education classroom to serve children with special needs. Another is for a special education teacher and general education teacher to combine the children in their classes (if small enough numbers permit) and share the teaching for ALL the children, relying on each teacher's expertise (Cook & Friend, 1996).

2. What staff development is suggested for teachers of inclusive classes?

Both special education and general education teachers must be given the needed staff development and planning time to provide for the needs and interests of ALL children they teach (Salend, 2001). Selected staff development issues relevant to successful inclusion include:

- curriculum, physical environment, and lesson individualization and modification;
- knowledge bases of specific special needs;
- adult collaboration strategies;
- family-school partnership strategies; and

- child-child social interaction guidance (especially to support interactions of children with special needs with typically developing peers).

3. What types of curriculums will best support inclusion?

A curriculum that individualizes learning for ALL children in the class will be most ready for inclusion of children with identified special needs. Inclusive classes have teachers who support, teach, and guide children, utilizing a wide range of available materials and a schedule that supports individual, small-group, and whole class activities. Families in these classes should be welcome partners in their child's education. ALL children will feel welcome if the teacher structures the learning environment to support ongoing interactions between children with and without special needs. This is especially important during times when children with special needs are transitioned into classrooms with their typically developing peers. Such interactions may not occur spontaneously without teacher support to guide children's social interactions (Lewis, 2003).

4. What types of assessments are appropriate for children's future?

Teachers will need to evaluate their teaching outcomes often, not only in terms of the typical A/B/C grade on an exam but also through other more authentic assessments such as portfolios to determine how well their students are able to apply their learning to real-life situations. Assessment tools should capture a child's performance and progress in communication skills, self-advocacy, and future work-related tasks.

CONCLUSION

Teaching should support ALL children's special talents and ALL children's special needs in an inclusion classroom. The benefits of children interacting with other children who are both alike and different from themselves include the development of an ethic of caring and team-work skills that are highly regarded in the contemporary workplace and in community relations.

RESOURCES

Allen, E. K. & Schwartz, I. S. (2001). *The Exceptional Child: Inclusion in Early Childhood Education* (4th ed.). Albany, NY: Delmar. This book synthesizes research- and field-tested practices in the field of early childhood special education to explore the context of inclusion of young children with developmental disabilities and the related family issues.

Bauer, A. M. & Shea, T. M. (1999). *Inclusion 101: How to Teach All Learners.* Baltimore, MD: Paul H. Brookes. The goal of this text is to introduce and walk a teacher through the issues and strategies for including children with special needs.

Cook, L. & Friend, M. (1996). Collaborate Teaching. *CEC Today, 3*(3): 12–13. Collaborative teaching models and the advantages of each are presented in this concise article.

Cosmos, C. (2001). Collaborating: Tips from a Teacher Who Walks in Both Worlds. *CEC Today, 8*(2): 2. This article shares collaborative teaching suggestions by an award-winning teacher of special needs children, Jayn Anthony.

Giangreco, M. F. (2002). *Quick-Guides to Inclusion 3: Ideas for Educating Students with Disabilities.* Baltimore, MD: Paul H. Brookes. Teachers are often told one day that a child with special needs will be joining their classes the next day; this book provides guidance.

Grenot-Scheyer, M., Fisher, M., & Staub, D. (Eds.). (2002). *At the End of the Day: Lessons Learned in Inclusive Education.* Baltimore, MD: Paul H. Brookes. Eight case studies illustrate how inclusion affects these diverse children. Coupled with research, authors take readers through choices of effective inclusive strategies.

Guralnick, M. J. (Ed.). (2001) *Early Childhood Inclusion: Focus on Change.* Baltimore, MD: Paul H. Brookes. With a the background of twenty-five years of research, this book provides insights into successful practices and concerns regarding inclusion of young children with special needs.

Kugelmass, J. W. (2001). Collaboration and Compromise in Creating and Sustaining an Inclusive School. *International Journal of Inclusive Education, 5*(1): 47–65. This article reports the story of one school's success with inclusion considering key stakeholders' commitment to learner-centered practices.

Lewis, R. B. (2003). *Teaching Special Students in General Education Classrooms* (6th ed.). Upper Saddle River, NJ: Pearson Education, Inc. This book provides insights into identification of children with special needs and recommended practices for successful inclusion of children from diverse backgrounds into general education.

Mayberry, S. C. & Lazarus, B. B. (2002). *Teaching Students with Special Needs in the 21st Century Classroom*. Lanham, MD: Scarecrow Press. This book provides quick answers for teachers wishing to create successful inclusive classrooms.

McLeskey, J. & Waldron, N. L. (2002) School Change and Inclusive Schools: Lessons Learned from Practice. *Phi Delta Kappan, 84*(1): 65–72. This article presents ten lessons to help teachers successfully work with children with special needs and those who are typically developing. The article provides reasons why the whole school should change to support this effort.

Nevin, A. I., Thousand, J. S., & Villa, R. A. (Eds.). (2000). *Restructuring for Caring and Effective Education: Piecing the Puzzle Together* (2d ed.). Baltimore, MD: Paul H. Brookes. This book explains the importance of collaboration and challenges that partnerships can overcome through examples of research-based strategies.

Salend, S. J. (2001). *Creating Inclusive Classrooms: Effective and Reflective Practices* (4th ed.). Upper Saddle River, NJ: Pearson Education, Inc. The individualized instruction research-based strategies in this book provide general education teachers needed strategies for children from diverse backgrounds. Themes of teacher reflective practice are consistent with NCATE standards.

Strieker, T. & Logan, K. (2001). Everybody Wins! *The State Education Standard, 2*(3): 26–31. This online article shares Georgia's successes of building capacity in schools to provide inclusive environments for a diverse population of children within the context of a standards-based curriculum (see National Association of State Boards of Education www.nasbe.org).

LINKING LITERATURE WITH MATHEMATICS AND SCIENCE

The integration of content areas is a major component of the Standards movement. Both the *Principles and Standards for School Mathematics* (National Council of Teachers of Mathematics, 2000) and the *National Science Education Standards* (National Research Council, 1996) note the importance of using literature in these subject areas. In an age when more and more is added to the school curriculum, the idea of implementing literature within the mathematics and science curricula can be beneficial for time management and for relativity to daily life.

WHAT IS MEANT BY LINKING LITERATURE WITH MATHEMATICS AND SCIENCE?

Numerous children's books present problem-solving situations and highlight how the characters resolved the issues presented. By introducing mathematical and science concepts in this medium, children are both intrigued and presented with ways that mathematics and science are experienced in the real world. Some of these books provide background in the history of mathematics and/or science, setting the stage for development of a higher interest in these subject areas. For example, when introducing the concept of geometry, *The Greedy Triangle* (1994), by Burns and Silveria, provides a high-interest story that includes vocabulary and concepts prior to the introduction of the geometry unit. Children's interest is hooked by the story. They are already actively involved in the new concepts to be introduced prior to the topic introduction.

The list below provides favorite children's books used by the authors on a continuing basis. In science, the true story about *Humphrey, the Lost Whale* (1992), by Tokuda and Hall, encourages children's curiosity about whales prior to the teaching of the science unit on whales. Humphrey's personality traits and characteristics are presented in a manner that intrigues student interest and involves them in a search for more information on whales.

WHAT ARE THE ADVANTAGES AND CONCERNS OF INTEGRATING LITERATURE IN MATHEMATICS AND SCIENCE CLASSES?

In addition to being recommended by national standards, school systems across the country are promoting the use of integrated curriculum units and teachers are expected to be knowledgeable in this arena. The integration of literature with both science and mathematics provides a unique manner in which to introduce new concepts and materials, while promoting time-management techniques. Stories are well received in classrooms across the country. A meaningful, well-written story that creates a link to a science or mathematics theme can provide a creative introduction to thematic units across grade levels. One concern voiced is that it takes time to locate quality books to use as an introduction. Yes, it does take time, but the professional journals in mathematics and science provide reviews of the best stories. The children's librarian at the local library is another excellent resource of information and the media specialist in the elementary school could be another resource. University professors who integrate literature into their curriculum are often more than willing to share their selections with interested teachers.

HOW DO I BEGIN?

First, select quality books that create an accurate concept of the unit to be introduced. Always read the books first to ensure that the content is correct and presented in a meaningful, realistic, and interesting manner. The resource list below is the author's quality-controlled list of favorites. Used over and over again, these books can create a treasure chest for you, the teacher, to discover and then share with your students. It is strongly recommended that you begin with one of your own top-of-the-list favorites to ensure enthusiasm in your presentation.

WHAT ARE SOME FREQUENTLY ASKED QUESTIONS ABOUT THE INTEGRATION OF LITERATURE WITH MATHEMATICS AND SCIENCE?

1. Where can I find the best books to implement?

The journal *Science and Children* (NSTA) provides a list each March of the best in Science Trade Books for children. This resource is current and a notable team of teachers has reviewed each book. Present a copy of this list to your media specialist and local children's librarian at the public library and you may soon find these books appearing on the bookshelves. The mathematics journal *Teaching Children Mathematics* (NCTM) has a literature section in each monthly issue. These two journals can be requested for your school library/media center.

2. Should I look for long books or short books?

As a general rule, a book that can be presented at one sitting is recommended. For older students, this may be extended to a longer book. It has been noted, however, that even older students enjoy the short stories that introduce a unit theme.

3. Are there any cautions about reading aloud in an introduction to a unit?

It is always recommended that the teacher read the selected book first before presenting it to the students. A book should always be checked for accuracy in content and for equity in words and pictures.

RESOURCE LISTS OF CHILDREN'S LITERATURE FOR MATHEMATICS AND SCIENCE

Concept of Number/Place Value

1. Friedman, A. & Guevara, S. *The King's Commissioners*. New York: Scholastic, 1994. The King discovers there are many different strategies to use for counting his commissioners.
2. Dee, R. *Two Ways to Count to Ten*. New York: Holt, 1988. A Liberian folktale, this story illustrates the different ways one can count.
3. Base, G. *The Water Hole*. New York: Adams, 2001. This beautifully illustrated story presents a counting book about animals around the world visiting a common water hole.
4. Giganti, P. Jr. *Each Orange Had Eight Slices*. New York: Greenwillow, 1992. This counting book presents creative ways to learn numbers.

Problem Solving

1. Viorst, J. *Alexander and the Terrible, Horrible, No Good, Very Bad Day*. New York: Aladdin, 1987. Alexander has numerous problems that urge the reader to provide multiple ways to solve them.
2. Base, G. *The Eleventh Hour*. New York: Doubletree, 1988. The intrigue in this creative story involves a mystery that older elementary students will enjoy solving.
3. Demi. *One Grain of Rice*. New York: Scholastic, 1994. Another mystery, this fable deals with increasing numbers and problem solving.
4. Thompson, L. *One Riddle, One Answer*. New York: Scholastic, 2001. A princess creates a clever riddle for her suitors to solve.

Geometry

1. Burns, M., & Silveria, G. *The Greedy Triangle*. New York: Scholastic, 1994. The triangle is dissatisfied with his shape and requests a change over and over again.
2. Tompert, A. *Grandfather Tang's Story*. New York: Crown, 1990. This is a Chinese folktale that uses tangram illustrations to highlight the characters.

3. Friedman, A., & Howard, K. *A Cloak for the Dreamer.* New York: Scholastic, 1994. Unusual difficulties arise when a tailor enlists the help of his sons in order to meet a deadline.
4. Paul, A. *The Seasons Sewn.* San Diego: Harcourt Brace, 1996. This is a historical story of quilts, shapes, and patterns.

Fractions

1. Mathews, L. *Gator Pie.* Littleton, MA: Sundance, 1995. Two young gators share a pie with each other and some noteworthy intruders.
2. McMillan, B. *Eating Fractions.* New York: Scholastic, 1991. This realistic book features pictures of children dividing food into fractional pieces.
3. Murphy, S. *Give Me Half!* New York: Harper Collins, 1996. A friendly discussion between siblings provides multiple ways to illustrate the concept of one half.
4. Hutchins, P. *The Doorbell Rang.* New York: Mulberry, 1986. Each time the doorbell rings, the children subdivide the cookies in a different fractional manner.

Weather

1. Barrett, J. & Barrett, R. *Cloudy with a Chance of Meatballs.* New York: MacMillan, 1978. This is a tall tale about a time when it rained juice and snowed mashed potatoes.
2. Hutchins, P. *The Wind Blew.* New York: Macmillan, 1993. Fascinating children of all ages, this story illustrates the way the wind works.
3. Polacco, P. *Thunder Cake.* New York: Philomel, 1990. To drive away a fear of storms, a grandmother tells a clever tale.
4. DePaola, T. *The Cloud Book.* New York: Holiday House, 1975. In this story about cloud types, the writer introduces historical ideas about clouds.

Environment

1. Cherry, L. *The Shaman's Apprentice.* San Diego: Harcourt Brace, 2001. This tale provides a picture of a young boy's life in the Amazon rainforest.

2. Cooney, B. *Miss Rumphius*. New York: Viking, 1982. This story is an excellent illustration of how one person can make the world a more beautiful place.
3. Van Allsburg, C. *Just a Dream*. Boston: Houghton Mifflin, 1990. After a dream about pollution devastation, a young boy decides to protect the environment.
4. Grindley, S. *Peter's Place*. San Diego: Harcourt Brace, 1996. Saving animals from an oil spill becomes a major project in this story.

Sea Creatures

1. Jacobs, F. & Kelly, L. *Sam, the Sea Cow*. New York: Walker, 1979. This is a tender story about the life of a manatee.
2. Tokuda, W. & Hall, R. *Humphrey, the Lost Whale*. Union City, CA: Heian, 1992. This touching true story of a friendly whale will peak children's interest in sea creatures.
3. Heller, R. *How to Hide a Crocodile and Other Reptiles*. New York: Grosset & Dunlap, 1994. Animals and their camouflage are the major points of this beautifully illustrated story.
4. Rand, G. *Prince William*. New York: Holt, 1992. Based on a true story of a little girl and her adventure during an oil spill, this book will fascinate all ages.

Butterflies, Bats, and Wolves

1. Cannon, J. *Stellaluna*. San Diego: Harcourt Brace, 1993. This is a tender story of a baby bat and her adventure that also contains factual information.
2. Ehlert, L. *Waiting for Wings*. San Diego: Harcourt, 2001. This is a colorful story that tells of the life cycle of a butterfly.
3. Fredericks, A. *Under One Rock: Bugs, Slugs, and Other Ughs*. Nevada City, CA: Dawn, 2001. A young boy discovers the many living things found under a rock.
4. London, J. & Van Zyle, J. *The Eyes of Gray Wolf*. San Francisco: Chronicle Books, 1993. This poetic text follows a night in the life of a gray wolf and illustrates his adventures.

CONCLUSION

Implementing the use of quality children's literature can provide an important connection between new content areas and reading for fun. Children's books are often the hooks to create enthusiasm about a new skill or concept and invite the children to participate in new learning.

RESOURCES

Burns, J. E. & Price, J. (September 2002). Diving into Literature, Mathematics, and Science. *Science Scope*, *26*(1): 15–17.

Burns, M. (1992). *Math and Literature*. Sausalito, CA: Math Solutions. This book provides important selections for beginning integration in the classroom.

Jacobs, A. & Rak, S. (November 1997). Mathematics and Literature—A Winning Combination. *Teaching Children Mathematics*, *4*(3): 156–57.

Mayberry, S. C. (1994). *Linking Science with Literature*. Greensboro, NC: Carson Dellosa. Science literature and related activities are provided here for elementary classroom use.

National Council of Teachers of Mathematics (NCTM). (2000). *The Principles and Standards for School Mathematics*. Reston, VA: NCTM. The mathematics standards promote the use of integrated curriculum.

National Research Council. (1996). *National Science Education Standards*. Washington, D.C.: Author. The science standards also highlight the use of classroom content integration.

Thiessen, D. & Smith, J. (1998). *The Wonderful World of Mathematics*. Reston, VA: NCTM.

MULTIPLE
INTELLIGENCES

The term *multiple intelligences* (MI) gained prominence during the 1980s and 1990s. Howard Gardner (1983) believes that every human being has multiple intelligences in varying degrees. This new view expanded on the idea of intelligence being expressed as only linguistic or logical-mathematical. Gardner originally identified seven intelligences: music, spatial relations, bodily kinesthetic, intrapersonal, and interpersonal in addition to mathematical and linguistic abilities. He later added an eighth: naturalist and has suggested that there are others. All eight of Howard Gardner's multiple intelligences are important. According to his theory, an individual may be gifted in one area without being outstanding in the other areas. As a result, teachers should not expect all students to learn in the same manner. He encourages teachers to structure lessons and activities within the classroom to include all eight intelligences and provide for individual student strengths. Teachers who know that children learn in different ways often seek to translate these differences into meaningful learning situations.

WHAT IS MEANT BY THE THEORY OF MULTIPLE INTELLIGENCES?

Howard Gardner (1983), in his Theory of Multiple Intelligences, proposed a new view of intelligence expanding the concept of intelligence. Gardner reiterates that the definitions of logic, reason, intelligence, and knowledge are not one and the same. His view of eight intelligences is much different from the traditional view of two intelligences: verbal and mathematical.

The key points in the multiple intelligences theory are (Armstrong, 2000, pp. 8–9):

1. Each person has all eight intelligences. These eight intelligences, however, function together uniquely in each individual. Most people are highly developed in some areas, moderately developed in some areas, and somewhat underdeveloped in the remaining areas.
2. Most people are able to develop each intelligence to an average level of competency. Gardner believes that everyone can develop all eight intelligences to a reasonably high level when provided with encouragement, enriched experiences, and excellent instruction.
3. These multiple intelligences work together in complicated ways as a rule. No intelligence exists by itself, but they continually interact with each other. People can exhibit strengths in an intelligence in multiple ways.
4. Multiple ways exist to illustrate intelligence in each category. There is no required list of attributes that one must exhibit in order to be considered intelligent in any one specific area. Individuals may show their gifts of intelligence in many ways within and between intelligences.

WHAT ARE GARDNER'S EIGHT MULTIPLE INTELLIGENCES?

Gardner's eight intelligences are as follows:
1. Logical-Mathematical: ability to detect patterns, think logically (associated with scientific and mathematical thinking);
2. Linguistic: a mastery of language, to express oneself poetically, use language as a means to remember information;
3. Spatial: ability to manipulate and create mental images to solve problems;
4. Musical: ability to recognize and compose musical rhythms and tones;
5. Bodily-Kinesthetic: ability to use mental abilities to coordinate one's bodily movements;
6. Intrapersonal: ability to know oneself and to understand one's own feelings;

7. Interpersonal: ability to understand the feelings and ideas of others;
8. Naturalist: shows an interest and concern for nature and the environment.

Gardner added the eighth intelligence in 1997, that of naturalist: interested in environmental concerns and interaction with varied species. Gardner states that each of the intelligences rarely operates independently.

WHAT ARE THE ADVANTAGES AND CONCERNS FOR ACCEPTING THE MULTIPLE INTELLIGENCES THEORY IN CLASSROOM TEACHING?

Gardner's Theory of Multiple Intelligences has several implications for teachers in regard to classroom instruction. The theory states that all the intelligences are needed to function well in society. It is advantageous for teachers to look upon all eight as of equal importance. Teaching should occur to a broader range of skills than the usual mathematical and linguistic. Another advantage is found when teachers structure lessons to engage most or all of the intelligences because this promotes a deeper understanding of the content material. One team of teachers (Sinclair and Coates, 1999) found that by administering a survey, students and teachers could identify strengths and weaknesses in learning styles and intelligences and implement the results in their plans. By implementing a wide variety of these strategies, students will have opportunities to work to their strengths while strengthening their weak areas. The most obvious concern is that these tasks require additional planning and time is a major factor, but the positive results in student learning and enthusiasm for learning are worth the effort.

HOW DO I BEGIN TO IMPLEMENT THE USE OF THESE MULTIPLE INTELLIGENCE STRATEGIES?

First, one should become aware of the eight intelligences and how they are defined. Next, begin to look for examples of each as exemplified in student behavior exhibited in the classroom. Gather articles, references, and websites that will begin to shed light on the implementation of this theory. Request information of peer teachers who may be enrolled in current coursework at a nearby university and who may shed some light on this idea. Then begin to collect activities that will relate to each of the intelligences. After implementing a survey to discover strengths and weaknesses in learning styles and intelligences, you can begin to implement activities that appeal to all eight.

WHAT ARE SOME FREQUENTLY ASKED QUESTIONS ABOUT MULTIPLE INTELLIGENCES?

1. What intelligences do students have upon entering the elementary classroom?

Gardner states that all students are born with all the intelligences. Students enter the classroom with different sets of developed intelligences; therefore, each has a different set of strengths and weaknesses.

2. What are some examples of teaching and assessment strategies that support each of the multiple intelligences?

Armstrong (2000) recommends the following strategies:

- Logical Mathematical: heuristic problems, scientific teaching, talking about numbers, and Socratic questioning (teacher serves as questioner);
- Linguistic: storytelling, brainstorming, and journal writing.
- Spatial: picture metaphors, color cues, and graphic symbols.
- Musical: songs, chants, rhythms, and raps.
- Bodily-Kinesthetic: classroom theater, charades, and manipulating objects.
- Intrapersonal: one-minute reflection, goal-setting sessions, and personal connections.
- Interpersonal: peer sharing, cooperative groups, simulations, and board games.
- Naturalist: outdoor activities, outdoor photography, endangered species activities.

For more detailed information on activities and assessment see Armstrong (2000) and Sinclair and Coates (1999).

CONCLUSION

The Theory of Multiple Intelligences, according to Gardner, illustrates the fact that children express their intelligence in multiple ways and with unique combinations of strengths. Implementation of activities that address multiple intelligences in the elementary classroom can entail a large investment of time in the beginning. Most teachers agree, however, that the end result is one that can lead to enhanced learning by more students in all of the content areas.

RESOURCES

Armstrong, T. (2000). *Multiple Intelligences in the Classroom.* Alexandria, VA: Association for Supervision and Curriculum Development. This is an outstanding book that clearly elaborates the theory of multiple intelligences and its approaches to teaching. Armstrong provides specific MI lessons in his appendices and provides excellent charts of ways students can exhibit their active knowledge in meaningful modes. Chapter 6, "MI and Teaching Strategies," provides even more information regarding strategies for each intelligence.

Brualdi, A. Gardner's Theory. (November/December 1998). *Teacher Librarian,* 26(2): 26–29. Explaining what the theory is, this article illustrates ways in which learning can be enhanced by knowledge of multiple intelligences.

Gardner, H. (1983). *Frames of Mind.* New York: Basic Books. An in-depth explanation of the theory of multiple intelligences and how it relates to learning and teaching.

Gardner, H. (1997). Naturalist as the Eighth Intelligence. *Sharing Nature with Children* (Spring): 1. After the publication of the book, *Frames of Mind,* Howard Gardner realized that an additional area of intelligence needed to be included.

Sinclair, A. & Coates, L. (February 1999). Teaching Multiple Intelligences. *Science Scope,* 22(5): 17–22. Implementing the theory of multiple intelligences in the classroom, these science teachers provide detailed information needed to begin application.

Sweet, S. (November 1998). A Lesson Learned about Multiple Intelligences. *Educational Leadership*, *56*(3): 50–52. Multiple intelligences can be successfully implemented using the knowledge gained from these practicing individuals.

Willis, J. K. & Johnson, A. N. (January 2001). Multiply with MI: Using Multiple Intelligences to Master Multiplication. *Teaching Children Mathematics*, 7(5): 260–69.

PERFORMANCE-BASED ASSESSMENT

Samantha and Ian are building a fort in the block center. Their first-grade teacher, Ms. Ortiz, has placed drawing and writing materials including a date stamp in the center. During the previous week's math and science lesson on force and balance, using the book *The Exploratorium Guide to Scale and Structure: Activities for the Elementary Classroom* by Kluger-Bell (1995), the teacher demonstrated ways children can plan and document the products they plan and create. Before Samantha and Ian started to build, they decided to make a blueprint, a way of planning by first putting their ideas on paper through a diagram of what their fort will look like. The teacher is anxious to see how they put this new skill into practice. Samantha looks at the blueprint and says to Ian, "I think the bottom of our fort is bigger than we thought, see (pointing to the blueprint)?" Ian says, "Let's make another part on that fort; an addition like we just put on our house (and draws an addition onto the original plan)." Then Ian writes "adishun" and stamps "September 22, 1999" over the part he just drew. Other parts of the fort blueprint are labeled with both invented spellings ("adishun," "batroom," "swimig pool") and conventional spellings ("kitchen," "living room," "play room"). Copies of this dated plan will go into their portfolios.

After they show their plan to the teacher, Ms. Ortiz makes abbreviated notes in her planning book for the following: "Tomorrow, during the morning literacy lessons, for the word study, have Ian and Samantha make some word family lists of double-consonant words (see swi*mm*ing and a*dd*ition).

Also, review the suffix '-tion' (see 'adishun' to show the spelling of the word, 'addition') and the consonant diagraph 'th' (see 'batroom' and show the spelling of the word 'bathroom'). Samantha and Ian chose to use a blueprint as a form of planning and documentation." She then makes a note to consider using this visual teaching and planning strategy in her next small-group math lesson that includes these two children and four other children. She also observed them using blueprints this week. Ms. Ortiz is pleased that both boys and girls are using blueprints as she strives for gender equity in science and math activities. This teacher understands these particular children's abilities and learning preferences by observing and documenting their performance. She then develops teaching plans according to their needs and interests, but also to challenge them to higher levels of understanding or new challenges.

WHAT IS MEANT BY PERFORMANCE-BASED ASSESSMENT OR AUTHENTIC ASSESSMENT?

This type of assessment is used to document how children perform a task or complex series of tasks and is to be focused on the obvious as well as subtle qualities of children's performance. Some of those qualities include: depth of thinking, critical thinking, creative thinking (imagination), time spent on task (pursuit), the kind of intelligence (see chapter 11) a child seems to rely on to perform tasks, and/or types and levels of questions the child asks. Performance assessments document samples of complex behaviors or skills that should represent probable performance on tasks in real-life situations and should be functional in the world of work. Performance may be measured while children are actually engaged in projects in context, that is, assessing child's processes and skills involved in making a bird house, including measuring and planning (Wiggins, 1999).

Some definitions equate performance-based and authentic assessments, while others differentiate these types. Those who differentiate suggest that performance assessment asks students to demonstrate performance on tasks, such as writing a passage or working out a number story problem in a testing situation. Authentic assessment goes farther to require that tasks be assessed in natural learning settings as part of the teaching and learning process, such as teacher anecdotal recording of children's processes used while working on a project or the products children create (Puckett & Black, 2000).

WHAT ARE SOME ADVANTAGES AND CONCERNS RELATED TO PERFORMANCE-BASED ASSESSMENTS?

Performance assessment assumes that children will be involved in their own assessment so children will be able to learn to self-monitor and guide their growth and development. Families will receive meaningful information to understand their child's progress. Each child's complete potential will be revealed through multiple means as children demonstrate what they know and can do, such as the blueprints created by Samantha and Ian. Performance-based assessment capitalizes on children's own construction of knowledge and can reveal each child's intellectual strengths. These assessments are more meaningful and timely as they are conducted in the context of children's learning environments. And because performance-based assessment is ongoing, planning can be based on day-to-day information about individual children.

While there are several advantages, constructing quality performance-based assessments requires teachers to acquire more technical skills to know what they are looking for and then know how to interpret performance to plan instruction to help children acquire needed knowledge and skills. Procedures used to collect performance indicators should be reliable (what is measured would be measured the same, even if measured by another evaluator) and valid (measures what it says it measures). This requires a high degree of objectivity on the part of the teacher who evaluates or requires multiple measures to confirm accurate reporting. And over all, performance measures are more time consuming than achievement tests or curriculum-based measurements.

HOW DO I BEGIN TO ASSESS CHILDREN'S PERFORMANCE?

- Consider what areas of child development might be needed to review to make informed and objective observations.

- Develop or locate an effective assessment plan and consider: (a) assessment purposes and goals; (b) what will be assessed and what child behaviors might be observed to determine developmental progress; (c) assessment strategies relevant to what is desired to know about a child; (d) who else might be involved in the assessment (i.e., teacher's aide); (e) places to observe the child's performance; (f) data (i.e., student work, checksheets, anecdotal records) storage and compiling; and (g) criteria against which assessment data will be measured.
- Start slowly.
- Use performance assessments at times and for certain assessments only, at first. For example, continue to use achievement testing materials, but transition use of performance assessment by adding one type for a few weeks, such as observation and recording during math time. Take anecdotal records of children's processes used with manipulatives and add this to their portfolios along with pencil and paper tests.
- Gradually remove some traditional testing materials with some performance-based assessment measures. Plan more of the work times utilizing activities that will provide information of children's performance.
- As teachers locate and become more familiar with certain kinds of assessments that fit their styles and give needed information, teachers can streamline documentations of children's progress.

WHAT ARE SOME FREQUENTLY ASKED QUESTIONS?

1. What are some assumptions that support the use of performance-based assessments?

Measuring what each child both knows and can do is based on certain educational assumptions about learning, knowledge, and teaching. Children learn through active inquiry and exploration with people and things, such as Samantha and Ian did with blocks. Knowledge is context dependent and certain meaningful contexts support knowledge acquisition. What Samantha and Ian knew about blocks was due to their repeated experiences in that block corner, but also at home with their own toys. Their home and school (contexts) include not only play things, but also include supportive and knowledgeable family members and teachers who guide and encourage them. Teaching should be sensitive to individual children's needs, interests, culture, family values, and unique learning styles.

2. What are some types of performance-based assessments?

- "Kid watching," informal, but informed observations of children in various learning situations can provide teachers and families information for planning and evaluation.
- Anecdotal records are accounts of significant events, such as when a child sounds out and spells a new word "kitchen" and a teacher records this action during or immediately after the event as evidence of that child's growth and change.
- Interviews, teachers' structure with specific guiding questions can illuminate details of a child's thinking beyond what can be merely observed. Diagnostic interviews help teachers plan specific content-based lessons.
- Directed assignments, with specific tasks, can be used to diagnose specific skills, style, and thinking.
- Games can provide teachers with information on children's progress with a skill or concept.
- Work samples from each child can be collected and analyzed to note patterns of behavior.
- Portfolios can be vehicles for collecting and analyzing selected artifacts that illustrate each child's emerging progress and processes used to master skills and achieve knowledge.

3. How can performance-based assessments be used to document mastery of standards?

Performance-based assessment is seen as intertwined with teaching and learning. Individual children's procedural (process of doing) knowledge as well as declarative (facts/information) knowledge is documented and compared to subject matter standards that children need to achieve. Performance assessment helps teachers plan multiple paths children can use to be successful at mastering standards. Performance assessment conducted by individual teachers can guide relevant instruction, while some entire districts or even states have adopted performance assessment strategies as their primary sources of assessment on student progress (Chappuis & Stiggins, 2002).

CONCLUSION

Performance assessment allows the child to show the teacher what he or she knows and can do under certain conditions and in certain contexts. Families can provide input into assessments, allowing greater participation in the teaching and learning cycle. Children also play an active part in their own performance assessment so they learn critical self-monitoring skills that they will need throughout their lives.

RESOURCES

Arter, J. A. & McTighe, J. (2001). *Scoring Rubrics in the Classroom: Using Performance Criteria for Assessing and Improving Student Performance.* Thousand Oaks, CA: Corwin Press, Inc. This book provides examples of scoring rubrics for real-world learning but also helps students see the value of their own performance.

Chappuis, S. & Stiggins, J. (2002). Classroom Assessment for Learning. *Educational Leadership, 60*(1): 40–43. This article supports teachers who use assessment as an instructional tool and involve students directly in their day-to-day assessment to help them self-monitor and improve their own progress.

Claycomb, C. & Kysilko, D. (2000). The Purposes and Elements of Effective Assessment Systems: Recommendations on the Foundations of State Testing Systems as Developed by the NASBE's Assessment Study Group. *The State Education Standard, 1*(2): 7–11. The study group recommended that states implement an assessment system that balances performance assessments with multiple choice items because the goal of standards is not to separate the "haves" from the "have nots," but to ensure that all children reach the standards.

Glatthorn, A. A., Bragaw, D., Dawkins, K., & Parker, J. (1998). *Performance Assessment and Standards-Based Curricula: The Achievement Cycle.* Larchmont, NY: Eye on Education. This book discusses the achievement cycle of using performance-based assessments to measure students' mastery of standards-based curriculums and then using those assessments to plan curriculum.

Haertel, E. H. (1999). Performance assessment and educational reform. *Phi Delta Kappan, 80*(9), 662–66. (Theme issue). This entire journal issue is devoted the potential uses of performance-based assessment for educational reform efforts.

Kluger-Bell, B. (1995). *The Exploratorium Guide to Scale and Structure: Activities for the Elementary Classroom*. Portsmouth, NJ: Heinemann. This a great book full of performance activities students can use to explore scale and structure principles used in building.

Puckett, M. B. & Black, J. K. (2000). *Authentic Assessment of the Young Child: Celebrating Development and Learning*. New York: Macmillan. This resource provides an extended definition of authentic assessment and illustrates several useful strategies.

Wiggins, G. P. (1999). *Assessing Student Performance: Exploring the Purpose and Limits of Testing (Updated)*. San Francisco, CA: Jossey-Bass. As the title indicates, this is an excellent resource for developing arguments for the use of certain types of assessments under specific conditions.

Wiggins, G. P. & McTighe, J. (1998). *Understanding by Design*. Alexandria, VA: Association for Supervision and Curriculum Development. This book lays out the foundation for starting with goals and expectations for student achievements as the basis for designing, implementing curriculum—a "backward" design.

PORTFOLIO
ASSESSMENT

It is important to set high standards in assessment practices because they play such a major role in teaching and student learning. Many educators view assessment as the typical Friday test and the standardized tests given each spring. But scores on these tests should be viewed as only one piece of the whole assessment picture.

WHAT IS MEANT BY PORTFOLIO ASSESSMENT?

Portfolios can provide teachers with valued information about students and how they learn. Portfolios are "systematic, purposeful, and meaningful collections of students' works in one or more subject areas" (DeFina, 1992, p. 13) over time, demonstrating progress in learning. Teachers need to know what is expected of them in the portfolio assessment arena. Portfolio assessment can best serve the purpose when it is one area of assessment, grouped with performance assessment, Friday tests, checklists, observations, and more.

WHAT ARE THE ADVANTAGES AND CONCERNS OF IMPLEMENTING PORTFOLIO ASSESSMENT IN MY CLASSROOM?

Portfolios provide students an opportunity to actively participate in the way they are assessed and to view their own progress over time. Portfolios can provide beneficial information for parent conferences as well as for the teacher in the next grade level. Anxiety is a major issue when traditional means of testing are announced. In portfolio assessment, students are able to illustrate their knowledge in a way that is comfortable, effective, practical, and meaningful.

Upon completion of a training module provided by the school, school system, or university personnel, teachers who implement portfolio assessment generally express positive feelings about this form of assessment. Though time consuming, the implementation of portfolio assessment is highly beneficial for students, allowing them to demonstrate their learning in a variety of nonthreatening ways. It allows students to showcase their knowledge with a project, poem, or mathematics lesson instead of using tests as the only form of assessment.

Lambdin and Walker (1994, p. 318) state three reasons why portfolios were implemented in their schools: (a) Portfolio assessment is a better way to assess the whole child than relying on test scores alone because it allows a variety of samples to be taken rather than using the score on one test; (b) Portfolio assessment helps students develop self-assessment skills in that it encourages them to continually assess and evaluate their own progress over time; and (c) Portfolio assessment helps establish better communication between students, parents, and teachers. A variety of student assignments and projects over time can be more meaningful and understandable to parents than a single test score.

Concerns about the implementation of portfolio assessment include:

- Criteria Selection. Often schools appoint a committee to ensure portfolio artifact selection (samples of student work) is uniform throughout the school or grade level. If left to the individual teachers, there can be great differences between portfolio assessments from classroom to classroom. General school guidelines are recommended that allow room for individual classroom creativity. For example, a school can designate required artifacts for each student portfolio, while providing students with an opportunity to select some of their own artifacts. For instance, the required items could be a reflective letter about the portfolio itself, one project, one writing sample, and one mathematical problem-solving activity. Other schools may choose to require only the reflective letter.

- Teacher Education. Teachers who succeed in portfolio implementation are usually those who have been thoroughly educated in portfolio assessment and those who support its use. The professor or peer-teacher should be carefully selected and the number of portfolio sessions should be multiple, rather than a one-time inservice. The school system or nearby university should have excellent sources to recommend for this training.
- Parent Training. Workshops (similar to those mentioned earlier for teachers) to involve parents in the process of portfolio assessment are an important piece of this process. Parents, who understand the idea and are provided an opportunity to have their questions resolved, can become enthusiastic partners in the portfolio assessment procedure and will better understand the student portfolios when they are presented.

HOW DO I BEGIN TO IMPLEMENT PORTFOLIO ASSESSMENT?

Begin using portfolio assessment with the strong support of your administrators. Your peers and parents can become willing partners in the portfolio process when you include them in the process from the start. The concept and the procedures of portfolio assessment should also be explained to your students. You may want to begin by stating that students are going to begin making important decisions about the evaluation of their work. Explanations about what portfolios are, the reasons for their use, and how the process works are essential parts of portfolio implementation. If possible, students, parents, peers, and administrators should be presented with examples of effective portfolios used in another classroom or school.

When you start, read everything you can find about portfolios, discuss portfolios with peers who are using them, have an organized plan, and start small with one content area. Explain your ideas to both students and parents, keep portfolios accessible, and share your enthusiasm!

It is best to begin small and in only one subject area. Explain that the purpose of a portfolio is to illustrate student growth over a given period of time. Next, discuss with the students the types of assignments that they may want to include. If you compare student portfolios to artist portfolios, students can begin to see how the process works. Artists do not include all of their work in their portfolios. Each artist individually selects only his or her very best work, knowing the work is representative of him or her.

Be sure to set up a schedule. It is recommended that you begin a pilot session of portfolio implementation for one grading period. In other words, start small by using a portfolio in only one subject area for six to nine weeks. Use what you learn from this pilot program to define your semester or year-long program, if possible. Students should know your expectations, what artifacts to include, when to include items, and when replacements may be made. Choose an accessible location for the portfolios and decide if they will be stored in crates, folders, or boxes.

WHAT ARE SOME FREQUENTLY ASKED QUESTIONS ABOUT PORTFOLIO ASSESSMENT?

1. What types of assessment materials are placed in portfolios?

It is important to require a detailed table of contents in the front of the portfolio. Items to be included in the portfolio may be essays and reports, letters, poetry, creative writing, problems and solutions, puzzles, journal entries, science projects, interviews, team projects, tests, teachers' comments, parents' observations, and so on. The list of accepted items should be ongoing.

Peer conferences (pairs of students) are beneficial to provide peer input into items selected and the reasons why they were selected. A few key phrases for use in selecting artifacts for the portfolio might be: favorite piece, best effort, most impressive, best problem-solving work, most creative, and the like.

2. Who selects the artifacts for portfolios?

Each student selects the artifacts for his or her own portfolio, with minimal guidance from the teacher. Each item selected should serve a definite purpose. When students make decisions about what is to be included in the portfolio and why, they are beginning to establish standards for the evaluation of their own progress. Students are encouraged to select their best work samples for inclusion in the portfolio. They may also, however, select an artifact illustrating something they did not understand only to include a later version showing their progress in that area.

3. What is a reflective essay?

It is strongly recommended that reflective essays be used in portfolios. There are numerous ways to use them. Have each student select five items and write an essay stating why those particular items were selected and how they illustrate the student's learning. Reflective essays may be written about certain artifacts, may be written on a monthly basis, or if the portfolio is kept small and selective, the reflective essay may be written for each item selected. The use of reflective essays requires the student to analyze just why the item was selected to represent his best academic progress.

CONCLUSION

Portfolios provide opportunities to assess daily, meaningful tasks; encourage conferencing between student, parent, and teacher; and allow the student to evaluate his or her own weaknesses and strengths. Teachers experienced in portfolio use relate that portfolios are time consuming and labor intensive, but they strongly promote understanding and learning. Because student learning is the ultimate goal, portfolios can assist in meeting that objective.

RESOURCES

DeFina, A. (1992). *Portfolio Assessment: Getting Started*. New York: Scholastic Professional Books. This is a teacher-friendly book that addresses how to implement your first student portfolio in the elementary classroom.

Lambdin, D. V. & Walker, V. L. (1994). Planning for Classroom Portfolio Assessment. *Arithmetic Teacher, 41*(February): 318–24. Discussing why portfolios are beneficial, this article reviews the research behind portfolio assessment.

Schurr, S. (1999). *Authentic Assessment: Using Product, Performance, and Portfolio Measures from A – Z*. Columbus, OH: National Middle School Association. The overarching theme of this book is the alignment of content area instruction and effective assessment. Ideas are presented to create more comprehensive teaching practices and assessments of student progress.

Seely, A. E. (1994). *Portfolio Assessment.* Westminster, CA: Teacher Created Materials, Inc. Guidelines for the construction of portfolios are presented in this book. Sample checklists and evaluations are also included for teacher and student use in the creation of an effective portfolio.

Stenmark, J. K. (1991). *Mathematics Assessment: Myths, Models, Good Questions, and Practical Suggestions.* Reston, VA: National Council of Teachers of Mathematics. The classic addition to any professional library, this book provides issues and answers that are beneficial in planning portfolio assessment on any level.

Sunstein, B. S. & Lovell, J. H. (Eds.). (2000). *The Portfolio Standard: How Students Can Show Us What They Know and Are Able to Do.* Portsmouth, NH: Heinemann. Guidelines to create a connected portfolio that reaches across curriculum areas are presented in this collection of articles. The importance of selecting artifacts and of writing thoughtful reflections is emphasized in the process.

PROBLEM-BASED
LEARNING

Research states that for learning to be meaningful it should be related to the real world of the students. That is exactly what happens when problem-based learning is implemented. In addition to the relevance of this learning model, it promotes a high level of interest and curiosity in the elementary school classroom.

WHAT IS MEANT BY PROBLEM-BASED LEARNING?

Problem-based learning implements learning experiences that begin with an "ill-structured problem" that could be a local issue, a controversy to be investigated, or a mystery to be solved. This type of learning challenges students to ask questions, seek related information from the past, present, and future happenings, and search for multiple solutions. Problem-based learning uses problems to invite students to branch into multiple disciplines to research and develop varied connections within the issues. It features three distinct parts: initiating learning using a problem, exclusive use of ill-structured problems, and using the teacher in the role of metacognitive coach to assist students in thinking about their own thinking.

Problem-based learning requires students to resolve problems rather than merely learn problem-solving strategies. Students learn to start with a question and a real-life situation and then learn to implement strategies and weigh alternatives. Students learn to think and act like scientists, mathematicians, and social scientists.

WHAT ARE THE ADVANTAGES AND CONCERNS OF IMPLEMENTING PROBLEM-BASED LEARNING?

There are many advantages to problem-based learning. Students are active participants in the learning and are vitally interested in the process. In the problem-based learning classroom, students are engaged and highly motivated. Research shows that student learning is increased when students learn by doing. Real-world connections are easily made using problem-based learning situations. Students acquire skills in critical and creative thinking (see chapter 6) and take the responsibility for much of their own learning while the teacher is the facilitator and guide.

This approach enables students to discover the history of the problem, to check on the present conditions, and to predict future developments and resolutions or solutions to understand the interconnectedness of life over time. Current issues can readily be found in the newspaper or be concerns that involve the school community as a group.

Concerns about the implementation of this type of learning infer that the time involvement is intense in order to select quality, appropriate problems for the grade level. Yet another concern is the time to prepare quality presentations for parents in order to obtain understanding and support for problem-based learning in the classroom.

HOW DO I BEGIN TO IMPLEMENT PROBLEM-BASED LEARNING?

1. Provide several examples of local problems of interest that need resolution.
2. Place students in a group and ask each group to identify one problem of interest and consequence.

3. Once a problem is selected, have groups use the KWHL process (K—what do we know, W—what do we want to know, H—How will we find out, L—What have we learned).
4. Have groups research the problem using investigation procedures, multiple sources, technology, and interviews.
5. Groups constantly revise the process of "What do we want to know" and the "How do we find out?"
6. Each group reviews the research.
7. Each group collects and evaluates data.
8. In conclusion, they formulate varied conclusions.
9. They come to an agreement.
10. Finally, each group presents conclusions or resolutions.
11. After the presentation, groups debrief to see what they might do differently next time.

WHAT ARE SOME FREQUENTLY ASKED QUESTIONS ABOUT PROBLEM-BASED LEARNING?

1. What are the goals of problem-based learning?

Most units focus on the following areas:

- To develop and retain an interdisciplinary content that promotes deep understanding;
- To develop and support expert problem-solving skills;
- To develop and encourage the use of self-developed learning strategies;
- To develop motivated lifelong learners with critical and creative thinking skills.

Implementing these goals, students learn to choose valid problems, weigh consequences and alternatives, and choose the best resolutions.

2. How did this idea begin?

Problem-based learning was initially designed for medical school students when it was discovered that they were graduating with quality information but without the critical reasoning skills to implement that information wisely. Recently, an effort has been made to incorporate these techniques into precollege education programs and elementary, middle, and high schools.

3. What is an ill structured problem?

Using an ill-structured problem is one of the key factors of problem-based learning. An ill-structured problem differs from the typical textbook problem in several ways. First, the initial problem statement lacks all of the information needed to find a solution. Additional information is needed. Second, there is no one correct way to approach the solution to the problem. Third, as new information is brought forth, the nature of the problem may change or be revised. Fourth, students may not ever gather all the needed information, but will have a deadline to make a decision based on the information that is in their possession. Ill-structured problems are frequently interdisciplinary, crossing subject area and content lines.

4. How do I identify quality problems?

- Search newspapers, magazines, radio, TV for interesting problems.
- Match the current instructional goals with the problem.
- Construct a web of all interdisciplinary concerns.
- Investigate and identify current stakeholders of the problem.

If all these can be completed, the problem may be one to consider for resolution.

5. What does research state about problem-based learning?

Because this approach begins with a problem and proceeds to a resolution or solution, this reflects problem solving in the real world. Research also shows that this type of problem finding and problem solving is related to creative thinking. Real-world problems also seemed to produce more creative responses, were highly motivating, and students felt ownership of their learning.

When questioned about this activity, student enthusiasm was high. Student assessment also reflected a high level of content learning and high-level thinking. Students have opportunities to write letters, interview, analyze data, read maps, and explain ideas to assess their problem-based learning. Problem-based learning inspired meaningful decision making and motivation while enhancing self-confidence. Teachers who implement these ideas need to invest worthwhile time and will require administrative support and staff development, but the result of the investment is highly rewarding.

CONCLUSION

Problem-based learning requires an investment of time and effort. Teachers report that both of these investments provide benefits for the entire classroom. Every town or city has problem issues to be solved. Involving students in finding active, quality solutions to recommend can enhance their studies and encourage good citizenship in the future.

RESOURCES

Burruss, J. D. (March 1999). Problem-Based Learning. *Science Scope 22*(6): 46–49. This article presents a summary of a classroom in which problem-based learning is successfully implemented.

Dooley, C. (June 1997). Problem-Centered Learning Experiences: Exploring Past, Present, and Future Perspectives. *Roeper Review 19*(4): 192–95. The reader will find interesting reading here on the history and the future possibilities of problem-based learning.

Gallagher, S. A. & Stepien, W. J. (March 1995). Implementing Problem-Based Learning in Science Classrooms. *School Science and Mathematics, 95*(3): 136–47. Science classrooms are an obvious place to begin the implementation of problem-based learning. The discussion of the benefits and concerns is highlighted here.

Lambros, A. (2002). *Problem-Based Learning in K–8 Classrooms.* Thousand Oaks, CA: Corwin Press.

Levin, B., Hibbard, K., & Rock, T. (Summer 2002). Using Problem-Based Learning as a Tool for Learning to Teach Students with Special Needs. *Teacher Education and Special Education, 25* (3): 278–90.

QUESTIONING
STRATEGIES

Asking questions is a natural behavior for humans that starts with a toddler's inquisitions—"Whas 'at?" Though an important vehicle for young children to learn about their world, incidental questioning is not the consequence of careful thought. Truly effective questions are not based on intuition, but they are carefully designed and planned for specific outcomes (Wilen, 1991).

Before reading the story *Goldilocks and the Three Bears*, intermittently throughout her story reading, and when she is finished, Ms. Crawford asks questions to stimulate children's involvement in the plot, characters, and the author's style. Ms. Crawford first holds up the book cover for all to see and then she asks a *divergent* question to draw them in. This provides a means for children to predict and reflect on possible events and then later compare these to the story plot. Ms. Crawford asks, "What do think is going to happen to the little girl and the three bears?" She writes this question on large chart paper so all can see. She waits three seconds until many hands are up, then calls on one boy who does not often raise his hand. He says, "Well, I can see that girl looks a little scared. Maybe those bears growled at her." Then he makes a growling noise, and other children join in and growl, too. Ms. Crawford writes this response on the chart, acknowledging this child's thinking. As other children provide other responses, she writes each down.

As the teacher reads on, she stops after reading the page that illustrates Goldilocks sitting at the table with a spoon in her hand ready to dip into the three bowls of porridge. She asks a *focus* question. "What would you have done, if you were Goldilocks?" All children's hands go up quickly. One very excited girl is called on and she says, "I don't know what's in those bowls, but my mom says to try at least a little bit of new foods. I would eat the stuff in the little bowl first to see if I like it, then if do, I would try the other bowls." Other questions Ms. Crawford asked throughout the story provide children opportunities to connect with the author's style and connect the author's intent with their own life experiences. She asked *clarifying* questions, such as, "Now how many of you know what to do when you see a bear?" To help them with numeration, she asked them a *convergent* question, "How many bears do you see in this picture?"

When the story ends, Ms. Crawford directs children to the chart paper full of predictions about the story. Children are asked to compare and contrast their predictions with the story lines. Ms. Crawford puts a Venn Diagram of two overlapping circles on the board with three *cueing* questions as headings for the sections. Over the left circle, the heading reads—What did you predict that was not in this story? Over the overlapping section, the heading reads—How were your predictions the same as the story? And on the right circle, the heading reads—What was in the story that you did not predict? These questions lead children's discussions of similar and different ideas as well as stimulate their recall of story events but would not have been as rich without the thoughtful questioning throughout the reading. The entire process allowed for more *evaluative* questioning to close the literacy lesson, such as, "What should Goldilocks have done when she saw the open door to the bears' house?" and "What do you do when you see other peoples' chairs or toys?" This story came alive because the children were not just listening, they were living it by responding to the words and pictures through thoughtful questioning (Harvey, 2001; Routman, 2000).

WHAT IS MEANT BY QUESTIONING STRATEGIES?

An effective question motivates student engagement by providing the right words and enough response time for students to compose a response. Great questions are crafted with attention to voice inflection, word emphasis, word choice, timing, the audience's (students') prior knowledge and needed challenges, the goals of a lesson, and the context in which the questions are raised.

WHAT ARE THE ADVANTAGES OF THE USE OF QUALITY QUESTIONING SKILLS AND CONCERNS ABOUT LESS EFFECTIVE QUESTIONING?

Teachers rely on intuition-based questions because they: (a) have not been exposed to a workable questioning strategy, (b) have not been trained to teach with such a technique, and (c) are not aware of evidence that incorporating such questioning strategies into their lessons will lead to increased student achievement or retention of knowledge. Research indicates that students of teachers who employ a questioning technique over those students whose teachers did not do so develop greater general achievement, problem-solving skills, creativity, and critical- and logical-thinking skills. Affective measures include increased motivation and participation (Van zee, Iwasyk, Kurose, 2001).

Effective questioning provides a form of assessment of learners' progress (Dantonio & Beisenherz, 2001). Educative, relevant, and appropriate scaffolding of questions can guide students to think about their own thinking (metacognition). Metacognitive activities can direct children to attend to particular aspects of information in lessons. These are the skills and abilities necessary for the careers of the new millennium.

HOW DO I BEGIN TO INFUSE QUALITY QUESTIONING SKILLS INTO LESSONS?

When implementing a lesson with effective questions (Chuska, 1995; Hunkins, 1995):

- Set the ground rules for question—answer exchanges (i.e., "All answers are accepted and not ridiculed.").
- Structure the questioning for students of all abilities, linguistic ability, and learning styles to succeed.

- Check and reduce excessive teacher-talk.
- Encourage the children to respond and not the teacher.
- Provide adequate time for children to think of a response (wait time). (Power, 2001)
- Self-monitor which students are called on and make sure to call on struggling as well as high-achieving students.
- Allow the motivation to come from the questioning itself, but you can use some sparse specific praise to reinforce or stimulate the question—answer process.
- Provide opportunities for students to develop and pose their own questions to increase opportunities for student thinking.

When developing a lesson plan:

- Consider also writing out or thinking through some possible question–answer–question interchanges.
- Use thoughtfully worded phrases with vocabulary appropriate to particular students. Thinking this through allows for adaptation of the type and form of question to the purpose for which it is asked.

WHAT ARE SOME FREQUENTLY ASKED QUESTIONS ABOUT DEVELOPING EFFECTIVE QUESTIONING SKILLS?

1. What are some of the types of questions? (Dantonio & Beisenherz, 2001)

- Clarifying—to gain more information.
- Convergent—with single answers; basic recall.
- Focus—to help students consider information needed to solve a problem or complete a task.
- Cueing—which may be used if children need help remembering key information; takes students back to previously learned information.
- Divergent—are open-ended, higher-order requiring analysis, synthesis, or evaluation and move children's thinking into the unknown.
- Interpretive—require learners to analyze how some thing or person impacts something or someone else; the consequences for information or ideas.

- Evaluative—which require students' use of information, but also social values.
- Reflective—stimulate conversation and examine basic assumptions.

2. What are some of the purposes that questions can serve?

- Managerial—reminding students of procedures or giving instructions.
- Diagnosing, checking, or reviewing prior lessons.
- Assessing students' level of understanding or interests.
- Getting interest, attention, or creating intrigue.
- Structuring and redirecting learning to consider other uses, adaptations, or changes in quality.
- Scaffold students' horizontal (more breadth of understanding or different techniques on a topic, such as learning how to read three letter words with short /a/, such as "hat" and "bat," then continuing on with other three letter words, but with short /e/ such as "get" and "wet") and vertical (increases of greater complexity or types of skills, such as counting before doing addition) thinking and learning.
- The questions posed will cue students to the level of thinking expected of them (Black, 1991).

3. How can the questioning be "stepped" up from lower to higher levels?

Behaviors at the higher levels of cognitive complexity including application, analysis, synthesis, and evaluation are most frequently required in adult life. Teachers who model and use this hierarchy of questioning have exciting learning communities! To sequence questions to guide students to higher levels of thinking (Chuska, 1995):

- Begin by asking lower-level questions and gathering information and helping children to recall prior stored knowledge. These help children to process information to make comparisons and contrasts, synthesize, make inferences, or explain.
- As needed, teachers may probe children with follow-up questions to elicit clarification, to redirect or restructure responses, or to solicit new information. Each probe should be only a small extension of the previous question.

- The highest step of questions should scaffold students' application and evaluation on new projects or new hypotheses (What if . . . ?).

CONCLUSION

Developing effective questioning strategies takes practice and thoughtful assessment of children's responses. All questioning does not have to be directed from the teacher to the children. In fact, a great deal of critical or creative thinking comes from ongoing question–answer–question sessions between teachers and children. Provide opportunities for children to develop and use questioning strategies—develop a questioning stance toward learning (Routman, 2000). Children may be able to provide the best insights teachers need to develop effective questioning strategies (Van zee, Iwasyk, & Kurose, 2001).

RESOURCES

Black, S. (1991). Ask Me a Question: How Teachers Use Inquiry in a Classroom. *American School Board Journal, 188*(5): 43–45.

Chuska, K. R. (1995). *Improving Classroom Questions: A Teacher's Guide to Increasing Student Motivation, Participation, and Higher-Level Thinking*. Bloomington, IN: Phi Delta Kappa. Children are motivated and engaged if classroom exchange is stimulating and when teachers respond contingent upon students' learning styles and specific needs.

Dantonio, M. & Beisenherz, P. C. (2001). *Learning to Question, Questioning to Learn: Developing Effective Teacher Questioning Practices*. Needham, MA: Allyn & Bacon. This is a comprehensive resource that provides examples of questioning types as well as history and research behind teachers' use of questions.

Harvey, S. (2001). Questioning the Text. *Instructor, 110*(8): 16–18. This resource provides strategies for children to think while reading, carrying on inner conversation, and for the teacher to stimulate that thinking through effective questioning.

Hunkins, F. P. (1995). *Teaching Thinking through Effective Questioning* (2d ed.). Norwood, MA: Christopher-Gordon Publishers. A comprehensive book about the nature of questioning, this resource provides extensive background to support an inquiry-based curriculum.

Power, B. (2001). Talk in the Classroom. *Instructor, 111*(2): 37–39. The author describes ways to ignite rich conversations and avoid the initiation–response–evaluation pattern of teaching.

Routman, R. (2000). *Conversations: Strategies for Teaching, Learning, Evaluating.* Portsmouth, NH: Heineman. The author develops a questioning stance toward learning.

Van zee, E. H., Iwasyk, M., & Kurose, A. (2001). Student and Teacher Conversation about Science. *Journal of Research in Science Teaching, 38*(2): 159–90. Investigates ways teachers can help children to formulate insightful questions and reflect on the responses.

Wilen, W. W. (1991). Exploring Myths about Teacher Questioning in the Social Studies Classroom. *Social Studies, 92*(1): 26–32. Author explores nine myths about questioning techniques, such as questioning does not require planning, and provides alternatives to myths.

RUBRICS
FOR ASSESSMENT

The word *rubric* has become a common vocabulary word in classrooms across the country. In order to promote fair, meaningful, and authentic assessment, the development and use of rubrics is encouraged. Students may have input into a rubric stating what they are expected to produce in any given assignment. Rubrics, when shared with the students at the beginning of a project, clearly state the expectations of the teacher and the student for a given grade. Awareness of expectations can be increased for each part of an assignment when rubrics are effectively implemented in the classroom. Assessment criteria should not be a surprise that a student encounters when receiving a corrected assignment.

WHAT IS MEANT BY A RUBRIC?

A rubric is a scoring tool that provides criteria to describe student performance at varying levels of proficiency. A rubric that is well written can help the teacher to score students' work more accurately, quickly, and fairly. It can also provide students with a description of the qualities their work should exhibit.

A rubric lists "what counts" and describes the variations of quality from excellent to poor. Students understand this type of description far more easily than merely a single letter grade of A, B, or C. When a student receives a C grade, he or she experiences disappointment but does not know what to do about it. The rubric describes the work expected for each assigned grade and provides information on how to achieve a higher level the next time. A rubric focuses on what the teacher expects the student to accomplish.

WHAT ARE THE ADVANTAGES AND CONCERNS ABOUT THE USE OF RUBRICS IN THE CLASSROOM?

Rubrics appeal to students and teachers for many reasons.

1. Rubrics are powerful tools for teaching and assessment. Rubrics lead to improved student performance by making the teacher's expectations clear and precise and by showing students exactly how to meet teacher expectations. Rubrics help to define quality.
2. Using rubrics, students become more thoughtful judges of the quality of their own work and that of others. Students learn to quickly spot and solve problems in the material presented. Using a rubric increases a student's sense of responsibility for the quality of his own work.
3. Rubrics shorten the time frame to correct student papers. One method is to have students use a rubric to complete a self-assessment and then present their work for peer assessment. Through this process, most of the difficulties can be discovered and resolved by the students prior to the teacher's assessment. Rubrics provide students with quality feedback on their strengths as well as areas for improvement.
4. The use of rubrics must be explained to the students, parents, and community. Once explained well, teachers usually agree that rubrics are beneficial additions to classroom projects and presentations. Rubrics, once experienced, are easy to use and to explain to students, parents, and fellow teachers.
5. The concerns that teachers voice about rubrics are that the creation of a rubric takes a considerable amount of time. The resulting improvement in the quality of student work makes the investment of time and effort worthwhile.

HOW DO I BEGIN TO CREATE AN EFFECTIVE RUBRIC?

An effective rubric should reflect the emphasis of the curriculum and the teacher's styles of teaching. In creating a workable rubric, students and teacher should become involved in the following steps:

- Look at multiple examples. Good and bad examples of rubrics should be reviewed. Identify the beneficial parts as well as those to avoid.
- List the criteria for quality work that match your grade level objectives. Brainstorm with the students. Be thorough in the description of the criteria.
- Describe the varying qualities of work. First, begin with the best and second, list the worst qualities. Then fill in the middle ground.
- Create a model rubric and use it for practice assignments. Evaluate the model after the practice. Incorporate the suggested revisions.
- Use self-assessment and peer assessment. Provide students with a task. Upon completion, ask each student to evaluate his or her own work. This is followed by peer evaluation of that work.
- Edit and revise the rubrics as needed. Use student feedback to make revisions in the rubrics.
- As the final step, implement teacher assessment of the rubric. (Goodrich, 1996–1997).

WIIAT ARE SOME FREQUENTLY ASKED QUESTIONS ABOUT RUBRICS?

1. What are the major tips in designing a rubric?

- List specific ways in which the students may meet each criterion.
- Avoid unclear language and generalities.
- Avoid the use of negative language.
- Keep it short and to the point.
- Select three to four categories of criteria.

Describing variations of quality within the rubric may be challenging. Heidi Goodrich (1996–1997) describes a successful technique borrowed from a fifth-grade Massachusetts teacher. This teacher describes her levels of quality as "Yes," "Yes, but," "No, but," and "No."

2. What is the history of the word "rubric"?

In the mid-fifteenth century, the word rubric referred to the headings in different sections of a book. This originated with the monks who, while reproducing sacred literature, began each new section of a copied book with a large red letter. The Latin word for red is ruber, thus rubric came to mean the headings for major sections of a book (Popham, 1997). Several decades ago, the term took on new meaning for teachers when measurement specialists used it to describe the rules that guided the scoring of student work.

3. What role does a rubric play in assessment?

Rubrics are generally used to judge performance-based assessments. They are not used to judge short-answer or multiple-choice tests. Rubrics help students increase their level of learning and tend to produce better quality projects. Rubrics should be given to the students prior to the assignment of the specific task. The use of rubrics appears to increase the chances that all students will do well on a given assignment. Students evaluate and revise their own work using the criteria described on the classroom rubric. The implementation of rubrics promotes student responsibility for each assignment. Students begin to understand the evaluation process and the quality of work that is expected for the task when rubrics are implemented in the classroom.

CONCLUSION

Teachers report that creating rubrics is time-consuming work. They do note, however, that rubrics are beneficial in helping students become more attuned to the characteristics of high-quality work and often lead students to produce the expected high-quality work. Rubrics illustrate concrete ways in which students can submit, revise, and improve their work to meet a high level of quality. They provide clear performance targets while promoting a focus on excellence.

RESOURCES

Arter, J. & McTighe, J. (2000). *Scoring Rubrics in the Classroom.* Thousand Oaks, CA: Corwin Press. This resource describes the varied types of rubrics and their effectiveness in the classroom. It describes ways to design effective rubrics and use them to improve student performance.

Goodrich, H. (December 1996–January 1997). Understanding Rubrics. *Educational Leadership, 54*(4): 14–18. The information presented here provides a readable background for beginning the implementation of rubrics.

Marzano, R. J., Pickering, D., & McTighe, J. (1993). *Assessing Student Outcomes.* Alexandria, VA: Association for Supervision and Curriculum Development. Rubrics as a form of assessment are highlighted as meaningful additions to the evaluation of student work.

O'Neil, J. (August 1994). Making Assessment Meaningful. *Update: ASCD, 36*(6): 1, 4–5. This quick overview of the changes that are occurring in the classroom emphasizes quality and precise assessment.

Popham, W. J. (October 1997). What's Wrong and What's Right with Rubrics? *Educational Leadership, 55*(2): 72–77. Rubrics can be a quality tool for use in the assessment of assignments. The right and the wrong way to implement rubrics are noted here.

Seely, A. E. (1994). *Portfolio Assessment.* Westminster, CA: Teacher Created Materials, Inc. This is a teacher-friendly book that provides guidelines for the development of rubrics and provides sample rubrics.

Stenmark, J. K. (Ed.). (1991). *Mathematics Assessment: Myths, Models, Good Questions, and Practical Suggestions.* Reston, VA: National Council of Teachers of Mathematics. A classic, this book clearly explains the reasons why rubrics should be implemented in classrooms.

STANDARDS-BASED EDUCATION: IMPLEMENTING REFORM

A ll around the country, educators, businesses, and citizens are working toward reform in education. The society of today demands that its workers possess the skills needed for this information age in which we live. The need for schools to implement change is necessary so that the needs of diverse students are met by the teaching and learning process. Today's students must know how to make important decisions and to locate, comprehend, and evaluate new information from a wide variety of sources. Today's workers must be able to communicate effectively and be critical and creative thinkers (see chapter 6). Education reform is necessary in order for students to keep up with a changing world. The Standards Movement is a major force in the field of education reform today.

WHAT IS MEANT BY A STANDARD?

A *standard* is a vision that reflects changes in society and in learning. A standard describes what teachers should teach and what students are expected to learn. Standards give direction and guidance to a nation with diverse school systems. These standards are expected to provide guidelines for determining which concepts are of the highest value for all children to learn to be successful in contemporary society.

WHAT IS MEANT BY THE STANDARDS MOVEMENT?

The current emphasis on the development of national standards goes back to 1989 when the country's governors recommended that America establish national education goals. Prior to that time, reports such as *A Nation at Risk* highlighted the need for more direction in school planning. *Goals 2000* became a reality and a plan was developed to meet these goals. The *Secretary's Commission on Achieving Necessary Skills (SCANS) Report,* which was developed by the Department of Labor, seconded the need for education reform. This Commission defined the skills needed for successful employment and suggested levels and manners of proficiency so that it could become a part of the learning of every student. This report, published in 1991, provided the basis for numerous state standards.

The document *Curriculum and Evaluation Standards for School Mathematics* is frequently referred to as the *Standards* and is used to inform curriculum. Published in 1989 by the National Council of Teachers of Mathematics, the *Standards* carefully reflect the need for reform in both the teaching and the learning of mathematics. The math *Standards* was the first set of curriculum content area standards to be published. One of the central themes in the math *Standards* is that all students need to learn more, as well as different mathematics, and that school instruction in mathematics must change in a significant manner. The *Standards* were written to guide the revision of school curriculum and evaluation in the area of mathematics. The *Standards* defines the following five general goals for students formulated by a team of leading mathematicians around the country and approved by teacher members.

Students should:

1. learn to value mathematics;
2. develop mathematical confidence;
3. become enthusiastic problem solvers;
4. learn to communicate mathematically; and
5. learn to reason mathematically.

These goals will enable students to develop mathematical self-confidence and to achieve mathematical power. They emphasize that learning mathematics is an active process, hence "knowing" mathematics and "doing" mathematics are one and the same. They also stress the implementation of technology as an important feature in all levels of mathematics classrooms. They reiterate that all students should have access to calculators and computers.

The *Principles and Standards for School Mathematics* (NCTM, 2000) highlights ten areas of mathematics to be included in all grade levels. These areas are: Number and Operations, Algebra, Geometry, Measurement, Data Analysis and Probability (the content standards), Problem Solving, Reasoning and Proof, Communication, Connections, and Representation (the process standards). The recommendations for implementation are provided according to the following four combination grade levels: preK–2, 3–5, 6–8, and 9–12. Other professional organizations in the areas of Science, Reading, Language Arts, Social Studies, and so on have also published standards for curriculum implementation.

WHAT ARE THE ADVANTAGES AND CONCERNS OF IMPLEMENTING A STANDARDS-BASED EDUCATION?

If students are to be content literate as well as productive citizens in the twenty-first century, they will need a quality academic background. The value of a standards-based education is that those necessary skills are brought to the forefront. No longer is a child being taught exactly as his or her parents were taught. Instead, standards-based education asks for a shift in what it means to teach in order to enable students to learn and not just provide information to them.

In order to accomplish this agenda, teachers need more long-term support and more opportunities for professional development. Not only does the curriculum require change, but so do teaching practices and student assessment.

A major concern about the implementation of standards-based education is that there are now standards in each curriculum area and often the national standards and the state standards are not adequately integrated for easy implementation in the classroom. Many states are currently integrating their state standards with the national standards.

Teachers express the need for more training on the implementation of standards-based learning. States now appear to be providing more guidance to their teachers on how best to implement these standards. It is of high importance for teachers to both know the standards and be trained in how to best implement them.

HOW CAN I BEGIN TO IMPLEMENT THE STANDARDS IN MY CLASSROOM?

The first task for the implementation of standards-based education is to become familiar with the national standards. At first, it is best to select one or two content areas and read the national standards as well as the state and local standards for those areas. It is highly recommended that you work with your fellow grade level teachers in the implementation of these standards.

Throughout this study, in every content area, the teacher should continually ask: Why am I requiring this assignment? Do students understand the reason? Are the activities that illustrate implementation of the standards quality activities? Clear, manageable grade level standards accompanied by sensible learning benchmarks and assessments can only enhance learning in today's classroom. They can help teachers realize the goal of quality learning for all students.

WHAT ARE SOME FREQUENTLY ASKED QUESTIONS ABOUT STANDARDS IMPLEMENTATION?

1. Implementing the standards seems to be an overwhelming task. How can I prepare during the summer to implement this idea in the fall?

In preparation for implementation in the fall, it is recommended that you determine which content area standards you will use in the first six weeks and set out to read the document from cover to cover. Next, gain as many current articles written by schools that have struggled with this issue so that you can learn from their implementation.

Finally, it is suggested that you pair up with a peer teacher and contact a nearby school that has already started this implementation. Debrief with a teacher in that school so that you have a clear picture of what can be effective in your classroom. Background research will help you prepare for your own standards-based education implementation in the fall.

2. Who can provide assistance if I need more help?

Each of the professional education organizations for the various content areas has a member services or information area. A phone call to any one of these groups will lead you to the best information and services on standards-based education. Articles in professional journals will help you to review what other schools have found to be helpful in the successful implementation of this idea.

CONCLUSION

Implementing standards-based education can add a new dimension to your classroom. Planning goals and assessment practices that fulfill state and national recommendations can lead to higher quality learning in the classroom. It is important to research these standards to see where the best fit is in your class. Working with a partner teacher or a team of teachers can make this plan successful.

RESOURCES

Burrill, G. (October 1997). The NCTM Standards: Eight Years Later. *School Science and Mathematics, 97*(6): 335–40. This is an excellent overview of the Standards Movement and how it has been implemented.

Grenhawk, J. (September 1997). Multiple Intelligences Meet Standards. *Educational Leadership, 55*(1): 62–65. Gardner's Theory of Multiple Intelligences is shown to be closely related to standards-based learning.

National Council of Teachers of Mathematics (NCTM). (1989).*Curriculum and Evaluation Standards for School Mathematics.* Reston, VA: NCTM. The first set of national standards published, this document provides a clear picture of the required changes needed for school reform in the area of mathematics.

National Council of Teachers of Mathematics (NCTM). (2000). *Principles and Standards for School Mathematics.* Reston, VA: NCTM. The latest newly revised national standards, this book is meant to be a resource guide for all teachers and administrators in grades preK through 12. This model promotes active understanding of important mathematical concepts and processes and provides ways in which students can obtain that understanding.

Oleson, V. L. (September 1998). Incredible Comparisons: Experiences with Data Collection. *Teaching Children Mathematics,* 5(1): 12–18. This resource provides a classroom overview of the implementation of standards-based learning in the elementary school.

Popham, W. J. (December 1997). The Emperor's New Education Standards? *Education Digest,* 63(4): 23–27. This article provides a commentary on the new education standards in comparison to existing standards.

Schmoker, M. & Marzano, R. J. (March 1999). Realizing the Promise of Standards-Based Education. *Educational Leadership,* 56(6): 17–21. The successful implementation of standards-based education is an ongoing process and a goal that continues to expand.

STRATEGIES FOR
DIVERSE LEARNERS

The life experiences each child brings to the classroom suggest the need for differentiated strategies that help students connect the new information learned in school with the range of skills each brings from home and talents each possesses. A class of first graders, for example, may range in age from six to seven years and their reading levels may range from emerging reader to expert.

WHAT IS MEANT BY STRATEGIES
FOR DIVERSE LEARNERS?

Visualizing instruction intended for everyone in the class comes easy to most of us as much of our own education may have included, for example, the teacher demonstrating addition on the chalkboard and then all students completing the same worksheet with more of the same problems. On the other hand, utilizing strategies to accommodate diverse learners' unique critical and creative thinking abilities, experiential knowledge, native language, culture-influenced preferences, gender-based preferences, learning style preferences, academic successes, and intelligences strengths (see chapter 11) requires some variation in:

1. the teacher's presentation style (i.e., have manipulative materials for kinesthetic learners or young students to learn to add; provide photos

or diagrams on the chalkboard to help students whose first language is not English understand a concept; divide students into teams consisting of students with a range of abilities and talents so members can support and complement each other during work on a group project) and

2. ways the students express what they know (i.e., tell a story or write a story; report the facts of a story or report on the inferences of the author of the story) (Tomlinson, 2001).

WHAT ARE SOME ADVANTAGES AND CONCERNS ABOUT THE USE OF STRATEGIES FOR DIVERSE LEARNERS?

Students' personalities have a great deal to do with their motivation for certain tasks or their learned social skills for taking part in group work. For some students, their cultural norms include a great deal of collaborative or shared activities, so a common school rule like "do your own work" may be quite unfamiliar. Understanding directions for an assigned task requires certain critical thinking skills (see chapter 6). Assignment directions may be presented in unfamiliar sentence structures or presented with questioning techniques (see chapter 15) or vocabulary that may not be used at a child's home or with peers in the neighborhoods, hence the child misunderstands or misinterprets and gets a poor grade on the assignment.

No matter how well planned a lesson may be, if there is only one way to perform a task (undifferentiated), quite often some students will be working ahead of the teacher's pace while others will be struggling to keep up, and still others have not made the connection between the lesson and the relevance to their learning preferences. Each student does not find the same avenues to learning equally engaging, relevant, and interesting.

HOW DO I BEGIN TO CREATE CURRICULUM WITH STRATEGIES FOR DIVERSE LEARNERS?

First, a teacher must step back and examine her or his own teaching and learning preferences and cultural and ethnic orientations (Hernandez,

2001). Are these strategies right for me, but not for some of the students in my class? What are these students' learning preferences and how can I plan different learning options and adjust the nature of the assignment to fit the learners in my room?

Understanding and accommodating students' learning preferences (or patterns) requires careful assessment of each student's:

- ways of processing information (cognitive style),
- preferences for performing tasks (i.e., in groups, alone, with music),
- what motivates each to perform tasks that do not come easily,
- approaches to tasks by different sequencing or organizing modes (whole to part or linear),
- level of precision each prefers (exact or can live with a few imperfections to add "character"),
- technical reasoning and creativity (comfortable working on projects requiring a high degree of imagination or prefers to work with known information).

One of the teacher's first steps to accommodating learning for diverse learners is to communicate high expectations for the success of all learners and to ensure that success can be achieved in different ways. The teacher's roles include:

- helping students reflect on their own learning preferences through a survey or through performance assessment activities (see chapter 12);
- setting up the physical environment to support learning and investigation in small groups, large groups, on the floor, and with a range of materials, including computers;
- enabling students to develop their own abilities and become self-directed learners by providing the skills they need to obtain the information they need (such as researching, study skills, or additional literacy development); and
- providing tasks or scaffolding that helps students see real-world applications to their own lives; to what they see as valuable to do with family and friends, to their school work, to their future career expectations.

WHAT ARE SOME FREQUENTLY ASKED QUESTIONS ABOUT STRATEGIES FOR DIVERSE LEARNERS?

1. Does providing strategies for diverse learners require that each student works on a unique task?

There are multiple avenues to learning and effective instruction that acknowledges students' gender differences, academic skills, and social and emotional strengths while reaffirming their cultural, ethnic, and linguistic heritages. Each student does not need to be working on a completely different task to accomplish this. Nor does the classroom need to be chaotic.

Selective grouping ensures that each student's needs and interests are met. Grouping all students with the same ability or strengths does not necessarily provide the support for their weaknesses (i.e., creative thinker, but poor speller). Providing flexible grouping that can change according to the type of work (i.e., grouping for math and other grouping for social studies, and another for project work) accommodates students with a range of abilities and allows for peer support while accommodating the rate at which each student completes tasks. At times it may be more effective to instruct the whole group (i.e., to start by reading a favorite book with information relevant to the lesson) but then at other times provide for small-group and individual instruction. In fact, whole-group activities can be valuable for students to come together to share their multiple perspectives, ideas, or products (Caldwell & Ford, 2002).

2. What are major adaptations or teaching strategies for diverse learners?

The following are a sample of research-based strategies teachers can use to accommodate all learners, especially the unique needs of linguistically and culturally diverse learners:

- Guide and monitor students to work together to support each other's strengths and mentor each others' challenges.
- Teach through a project approach or interdisciplinary approach in which students have opportunities to use (perform) and demonstrate their understandings in multiple ways, that is by writing, putting on a play, or creating a work of art. Then help students design an assessment

portfolio of collections of their work that captures their unique readiness, interest, and learning profiles (see chapter 13).

- Promote home/school partnerships that help students and families see the connection between work and school, but also helps the teacher see the important contributions families make to the holistic learning processes and products.

- Help students learn and use different strategies for memorizing information, for example, chunking information into reasonable pieces, use of music and rhyme, and mind mapping to organize stored information for easier retrieval.

- Engage students in questioning strategies (see chapter 15) that spark interest in learning and also guide students to generate their own questions and lead their own discussions.

- Help students plan and carry out activities that suit their individual readiness and interest similarities as well as differences, use choice boards listing the range of available activities or learning centers.

- Capitalize on students' cultural backgrounds and the richness of their native language, making their interests and needs a central part of the curriculum and bring needs, skills, and knowledge into students' agendas rather than trying make the children always fit into a set agenda. Before lessons begin, ask, "What do you know (about the lesson topic), What do you want to learn?" and then following the lesson, help students gather "What they did learn." At times provide opportunities for the learning experience in their native language with help from an interpreter, so all students can engage in learning a new language (Gay, 2002; Scott, 2002).

- Use cross-age tutoring or computer-assisted learning to get the individualized help certain students may need. Both the tutor and the child being tutored benefit. The tutor learns valuable leadership skills and experiences differing cultural norms, while the child being tutored gets the needed one-on-one help from a child more knowledgeable in a certain subject or skill. Many students identify with peers more easily than adults. Some entire schools have adopted a nongraded or multiage arrangement that supports continuous cross-age collaboration (Peters, 2000).

- Provide high-tech access. Students in today's high-tech world may also find the computer a helpful and engaging tool. Students who may otherwise not respond to conventional lecture teaching may find learning easier by interacting with a computer.

CONCLUSION

Teachers can attend to curricular mandates while also attending to students' diverse learning styles by considering ways that curriculum can be taught considering students' readiness, interest, and learning preferences. Effective teachers of diverse learners are personally committed to achieving equity for all students and believe they can make a difference in ALL students' learning.

RESOURCES

Caldwell, J. & Ford, M. P. (2002). *Where Have All the Bluebirds Gone?: How to Soar with Flexible Grouping.* Portsmouth, NH: Heinemann. This book provides alternatives to grouping only by ability and shares the strengths and challenges to each type of grouping.

Cole, R. W. (Ed.). (1995). *Educating Everybody's Students: Diverse Teaching Strategies for Diverse Learners.* Alexandria, VA: Association for Supervision and Curriculum Development. Recognizing the diverse cultural and linguistic populations in contemporary classrooms, this book supplies teachers with theory, research, and practical suggestions.

Cole, R. W. (Ed.). (2000). *More Strategies for Educating Everybody's Students.* Alexandria, VA: Association for Supervision and Curriculum Development. This book expands Cole's first book to include strategies for teaching history, civics, geography, history, and science. This second edition provides more coverage of populations underserved by schools.

Gay, G. (2002). *Culturally Responsive Teaching: Theory, Research, and Practice.* New York: Teachers College Press. The author presents compelling evidence of development in underachieving children of color when culturally responsive teaching is implemented.

Hernandez, H. (2001). *Multicultural Education: A Teacher's Guide to Linking Context, Process, and Content* (2nd Ed.). Upper Saddle River, NJ: Pearson Education, Inc. This book uses contemporary research to illustrate the effects of social and cultural factors on education, then provides concrete strategies to implement a multicultural approach to education.

Peters, D. (2000) *Taking Cues from Kids: How They Think; What to Do about It*. Portsmouth, NH: Heinemann. Curriculum designed around learner needs and interests is presented through the journaling of a teacher in a multiage-multiethnic class with her student teachers.

Sapon-Shevin, M. (2000–2001). Schools Fit for All. *Educational Leadership, 58*(4): 34–39. This article provides support for culturally sensitive practices that also provide for inclusion of children with disabilities. The author makes recommendations for changes in teacher education, school climate, and pedagogy.

Scott, S. (2002). Diversity and the Structure of Public Education. *The State Education Standard, 3*(1), 25–29. The author points out how the "industrial model" for schooling does not foster flexibility and innovation that is needed for diverse learners to improve their performance.

Tomlinson, C. A. (1999). *The Differentiated Classroom: Responding to the Needs of All Learners*. Alexandria, VA: Association for Supervision and Curriculum Development. This book provides clear, practical suggestions to extend content from the book *How to Differentiate Instruction* by the same author.

Tomlinson, C.A. (2001). *How to Differentiate Instruction in Mixed-Ability Classrooms* (2nd Ed.). Alexandria, VA: Association for Supervision and Curriculum Development. This is a second edition of a popular compact version of descriptions about what differentiated curriculum is and is not. Chapters provide insights into several variables teachers might consider when varying the curriculum.

TECHNOLOGY
INTEGRATION

After their research trip to the local pond, students in a fifth-grade class learned how to graph the data they collected on their laptops. The first grade also went on that trip and when they got back to class, some students used software to reconstruct the events and their findings through pictures and labels that are narrated by their voices. Other first graders searched CD-ROM encyclopedias to identify the frogs they observed. The local pond had been experiencing some changes in flora and fauna and children in this school are working with the local naturalist to determine the causes of these changes.

WHAT IS MEANT BY INTEGRATING
EDUCATIONAL TECHNOLOGY?

"Only when computers are integrated into the curriculum as a vital element for instruction and are applied to real problems for a real purpose, will children gain the most valuable computer skill—the ability to use computers as natural tools for learning" (Shade & Watson, 1990, p. 375). Technology should be integrated into the regular routine at the very beginning of the day, when students arrive and log in their lunch choice on the computer and can be used throughout the day to teach, guide, and assess students' learning. Technology is used in the classroom in four basic ways: (a) to bring important problems to the classroom; (b) to provide resources and scaffolds to enhance student learning; (c) to provide opportunities for feedback, reflection, and revision; and (d) to connect teachers and students to homes, to communities, and to the world! (Dede, 1998; Roblyer, 2003a, 2003b).

Technology integration is evident when the goals of the curriculum and the technology are coordinated—when students are using technology tools to expand their intellectual tools that help them assemble and construct knowledge. While physical manipulatives are important initial learning experiences, with computer graphics, students can explore new avenues and perspectives of, for instance, shape and color through software that stretches, pulls, and groups rapidly in exciting new dimensions beyond the physical world (Jonassen, Howland, Moore, Marra, 2003).

Technology such as multimedia software can support integrated, theme-based projects that require students' use of higher analytic thinking skills and greater depth and coverage of curriculum content. Small groups or pairs learn to cooperate on thematic tasks as, for example, one student searched the Internet for "Frog sites," while the other researched an amphibian book for potential frog names to use in the "key word" searches. The pair may collaborate further by sending an email to another student with a similar interest who is in a town over 1,000 miles away (Newby, Stepich, Lehman, Russell, 2000)!

WHAT ARE THE ADVANTAGES AND CONCERNS THAT IMPACT INTEGRATING EDUCATIONAL TECHNOLOGY?

- Selected technology uses can appeal to children with a range of learning styles and hence increase motivation and increased academic success.
- Skillful use of technology that supports learning (i.e., by being an on-the-spot resource of information or skill-builder) can move the learning responsibilities away from the teacher to be more student-centered and initiated.
- Students can work on much more complex assignments if technology is used to process labor-intensive mathematical calculations, leaving students free for the creative and critical thinking tasks (see chapter 6).

- Through the use of a multimedia presentation, students can develop more confidence in their verbal and written presentation skills; the computer "shares the stage" with the student and reduces some of the tension of getting up in front of peers and adults.
- Children who cannot yet read can enhance their skills as computers verbalize the printed words on the screen.
- Children with special needs, especially those with motor challenges to writing, can use adaptive technology to, for example, present their ideas in written form or perform mathematical calculations.

While there are many advantages, some concerns and challenges to providing meaningful and engaging use of technology exist. These include:

- Children in each class come to school with a wide range of technology skills depending on the availability of a computer in their home (due to economics or family preference), which could challenge the implementation of lessons that infuse the use of technology.
- Teachers may resist the infusion of technology and perceive technology use as a loss of instructional time with children.
- Teachers must receive the kinds of meaningful (relevant to their own curriculum) and ongoing technical training and technical support to be sufficiently comfortable to truly infuse technology tools and just add on technology use as another isolated subject. This also assumes that teachers have ownership in and choice of the materials used for integration; those they will actually use because these support their curriculum and teaching style.
- Without adequate staff development, computers may be used for solitary learning and impersonal interaction, rather than cooperative learning activities that utilize technology tools to support interactions and group processing.
- Administrators and school boards need to provide appropriate financial support for new materials and have a plan for continuous hardware and software upgrades.
- Adequate technology support personnel must be available to support teachers as they implement new uses of technology within their cur-

riculum or teachers will abandon technology resources or dismiss this as "just another fad."

HOW DO I BEGIN TO INTEGRATE TECHNOLOGY INTO THE CURRICULUM?

- To get started, choose one area of study, learning center, thematic project time, reading block, or other activity in the daily schedule.
- Consider the available technological expertise and then consider which technology skills would best facilitate the content learning and other skills intended for that chosen activity.
- Consider how to integrate technology into that activity. What software and what form of technology would be able to enhance children's meaning-making better than other tools? What other hardware might be needed? How much teacher-time will this activity take to guide and scaffold students' use before they can use it independently? How will the children's learning and the format of the activity be evaluated for the purpose of adjusting and refining teaching?
- Go ahead and try it.
- Evaluate, fine-tune the activity, and reteach skills to individual children as needed. Debrief with another teacher who may also be trying out some new technology, so reflect together. A partner brings another perspective to work through challenges and to celebrate successes. The next time this form of technology is used, both teachers will know what to expect.

WHAT ARE SOME FREQUENTLY ASKED QUESTIONS ABOUT TECHNOLOGY INTEGRATION?

1. Does technology integration mean a whole new way of teaching?

Classes should be child centered, based on the research of best practice, but also knowledge centered with a solid grounding in the traditional disciplines such as mathematics, sciences, social studies, and literature. Teachers and administrators guide students who conduct sustained research and inquiry on important problems by employing a wide range of modern technologies.

2. How does integrating technology affect children's thinking?

Students learn from thinking in meaningful ways. Meaningful learning requires meaningful real-life tasks like the ones they experience outside of school. Computers are tools with which students engage to access information and interpret and organize their knowledge. Carefully selected computer applications have the potential to extend and enrich students' thinking in creative, critical, and even more complex ways than with other tools. But of course, the tools alone would not be enough. Teachers who have received meaningful and supported staff development with technology must mediate and scaffold children's interface with hardware and software (Dockstader, 1999; Renwick, 1999).

3. How can the physical arrangement of the classroom support technology integration?

Teachers who truly want to integrate technology into their lessons must have computers and other hardware in their classrooms. Workstations with two to three computers on tables that seat a team of five to six students is one desired physical arrangement. Computer skills cannot be taught in isolation in labs "down the hall." Nor should computers only be put in a center as an "extra activity" when all other work is completed.

CONCLUSION AND TIPS

- A logical and systematic model of instruction, such as "model, practice, apply," provides an understood, shared context for students and teachers who will be continually trying out new forms of technology as more come on the market every day.
- Review local and national standards (i.e., ISTE, www.iste.org) designed to guide the developmental progress of students' computer skills and knowledge.
- Ensure that expected technology skills directly relate to the content areas and to the classroom assignments.

- Teachers, administrators, and families play important roles in selecting and evaluating the kinds of software that is beyond "skill and drill" and that can help students play and discover concepts and cause and effect relationships. Software reviews should also consider positive representation of gender, cultural, and linguistic diversity; the level of violence (i.e., blowing up mistakes); and the child's skills required to run the software.

- Make sure computer use is equitable. Make sure girls as well as boys are encouraged to use computers by, for example, selecting software based on their interests. Ensure that children who do not have access to computers at home have more access to computers at school. For children with special needs, look into acquiring assistive hardware and software technology to, for instance, augment sensory input, reduce distractions, and enhance memory.

- Because many families feel inadequately prepared to assist their child with a computer at home, consider offering Internet or evening courses for family members. Bringing the families and community along in the cybernet journeys can only enhance children's home-school connection.

RESOURCES

Dede, C. (Ed.). (1998). *ASCD Yearbook 1998: Learning with Technology.* Alexandria, VA: Association for Supervision & Curriculum Development. This edited volume includes chapters from several authors on issues related to including technology in the curriculum.

Dockstader, J. (1999). Teachers of the 21st Century Know the What, Why, and How of Technology Integration. *THE Journal: Technical Horizons in Education, 26*(6): 73–74. Teachers entering the schools are increasingly more proficient with technology; they are teaching through computers, not about computers. See: www.thejournal.com.

Jonassen, D. H., Howland, J., Moore, J., & Marra, R. M. (2003). *Learning to Solve Problems with Technology: A Constructivist Perspective* (2nd ed.). Upper Saddle River, NJ: Prentice Hall. Computers are tools that can be used as children and adults construct understandings and develop skills. This text shares how computer software applications can be used to learn school subjects and think through projects and problems.

National Association for the Education of Young Children. (1996). *NAEYC Position Statement: Technology and Young Children Ages Three through Eight.* While computers are popular, this position statement provides constructive suggestions to guide appropriate use with young children, preschool to third grade. See: www.naeyc.org.

Newby, T. J, Stepich, D. A., Lehman, J. D., & Russell, J. D. (2000). *Instructional Technology for Teaching and Learning: Designing Instruction, Integrating Computers, and Using Media* (2nd ed.). Upper Saddle River, NJ: Prentice Hall. Through a learner-centered approach, authors provide methods and design principles integrating technology into lessons to enhance learning.

Pioneer New Media. (2001). Integrating Technology & Curriculum: Florida District Employs DVD to Enhance Classroom Experience. *THE Journal: Technical Horizons in Education, 28*(7) (www.thejournal.com). Through a grant, this school district in Florida supplied teachers with DVD players and training in technology to successfully enhance the learning of children from low-income families in that district.

Renwick, L. (1999). Weaving in Technology. *Instructor, 111*(2): 83–85. This article provides advice to teachers on integration of technology into their lessons, such as how to conduct student group projects and helpful websites.

Roblyer, M. D. (2003a). *Integrating Educational Technology into Teaching* (3rd ed.). Upper Saddle River, NJ: Prentice Hall. Through a blend of theory and practice, this book provides both the novice and experienced teacher ideas for integrating technology into lessons.

Roblyer, M. D. (2003b). *Integrating Technology across the Curriculum: A Database of Technology Integration Ideas* (2nd ed.). Upper Saddle River, NJ: Prentice Hall. This dual-platform CD contains over 500 field-tested K–12 lessons that integrate technology.

Shade, D. D. & Watson, J. A. (1990). Computers in Early Education: Issues Put to Rest, Theoretical Links to Sound Practice, and the Potential for Contribution to Microworlds. *Journal of Educational Computing Research, 6*(4): 375–92. Concerns about the potential uses of computers by young children are dismissed with theoretical supports.

Sharp, V. F., Levine, M. G., & Sharp, R. M. (2002). *The Best Web Sites for Teachers* (5th ed.). Eugene, OR: International Society for Technology in Education. This is a classroom resource of over 1,200 websites, some of which contain lessons for integrating technology into lessons. See: www.iste.org.

THEMATIC APPROACH

P lanning using a thematic approach organizes learning around a central theme, such as the study of "bears" or "the pioneers." Based on the theme topic, issue, or problem, lessons or activities are connected. The planning process takes a system's perspective, with each lesson building on or extending others and each activity helping children understand another dimension of that theme (i.e., the number of black bears that live in the Appalachian Mountains in Pennsylvania; what the black bears eat; searching on the Internet for stories of black bears who wandered into people's yards; and writing a poem about a mother bear and her cub). When planning activities for the theme, a teacher keeps in mind specific goals or standards that need be mastered in each discipline, yet creatively plans relevant and interesting interdisciplinary (including more than one discipline) activities for students that imbed those standards.

WHAT IS MEANT BY THE THEMATIC APPROACH TO TEACHING?

Well-organized and sequenced strategies and activities are used to expand particular concepts that relate to a broad topic or theme. Students develop the skills they need while working on activities and projects. Each teacher decides if all lessons and activities throughout the day will be based on the theme or if only part of the day will be based on theme activities. Theme-related activities at selected times in the daily planning with some single-subject study periods (i.e., intensive reading blocks of two hours in the morning) is another option.

Thematic units can last from a week (such as theme about the circus during the week it is in town) to several weeks (such as theme on the beach for children who live in Miami). Activities can be interdisciplinary and should allow multiple opportunities for children to make natural connections between subjects or content by dealing with real-life concerns. When studying the beach, for example, children can count shells (math), chart the weather patterns (science), and study the history of the Spanish-speaking people who first inhabited Miami. While each example activity about the beach (above) is directed to a main subject area, each activity also requires the skills of other disciplines. For example, when children chart the weather, they use measurement skills to calculate wind velocity and use language arts skills to write a report about weather patterns. Some children may even choose to dramatize a TV newscast to illustrate how meteorologists report on the information they chart.

WHAT ARE THE ADVANTAGES AND CONCERNS ABOUT THE USE OF THEMATIC UNITS?

Learning through personally meaningful instructional strategies and through a variety of materials facilitates comprehension and creates an increased desire to learn more about the theme or topic. Through this process, students can develop and pursue their own interests through learning style preferences (see chapter 18). Students can also utilize an extended period of time to delve into a concept in depth. Thematic learning experiences also provide opportunities to make connections between previous learning and any new information. Students say, "We like what we are doing so we are motivated to learn more. We remember the information because this was interesting to us!"

By teachers giving students more responsibility for their own learning, students become independent problem solvers and thinkers. Teachers can help set the stage for life-learning if they help students learn the skills to find out what they need to know and learn rather than always expecting the curriculum to teach it to students. Other advantages and challenges to using thematic units include:

1. If the school is structured into subject-area time segments, the time periods can be combined to allow for more integrated learning experiences in longer time periods.
2. If the curriculum is departmentalized and teachers are each responsible for a subject, teachers could plan their lessons together to ensure their lessons coordinate across the subjects.
3. Standardized test scores are not negatively affected by thematic teaching, if teachers carefully infuse needed concepts and skills into the theme activities.
4. Themes do take time to develop, but there are many published resources on the market that teachers can use for thematic activities.
5. If basal reading texts are required, theme activities that supplement those reading materials and extend the reading to other subjects could be used.
6. Some theme activities will not be able to include every subject, but other theme activities can be used to ensure all subjects are covered at some time during the unit.
7. Make sure themes are the right size for the topic, issue, or problem. A minitheme such as the origin of St. Patrick's Day might last a day, while some themes, such as bones and skeletons, might last a week or two. A few themes such as the study of an entire continent might last for a month.

HOW DO I BEGIN TO DEVELOP A THEMATIC UNIT?

Choosing a theme or topic of study is the teacher's first step. The teacher might choose a topic based on an issue or idea in which several children in the class have shown interest or it may come from a topic required by the district or national standards (see chapter 17). In some cases, to select a theme, the teacher has the opportunity to brainstorm with the children on topics of interest. Themes based around science topics such as simple machines and social studies topics such as Native Americans have broad applications. Issues and problems, such as "How can we save energy at our school?" as themes create opportunities for students to understand and then solve a problem. The following are questions that guide theme selection:

1. If the theme is to be infused into the entire curriculum, then consider: Is the theme usable across all subject areas?
2. Is the theme appropriate and relevant to this age group of children?
3. Is this theme capable of including content and skills these children need to know and are able to do?

Using a thematic-webbing process is the second step. A web is a way of helping children see connected ideas and activities. This resembles the image of a spider web that has a central point—the theme with branches of related ideas extending from the center. The teacher can begin by placing the theme in the middle of a large piece of paper, then guide children with questions and clues to think of ideas or questions related to the theme (see figure 20.1).

The teacher's next step is to develop unit objectives while compiling activities and planning related field trips that connect the issues of interest to children and cover needed concepts and skills. Older elementary students can plan activities with the teacher.

WHAT ARE SOME FREQUENTLY ASKED QUESTIONS ABOUT THEMATIC UNITS?

1. What roles do students and the teacher play in the process of creating and carrying out a theme?

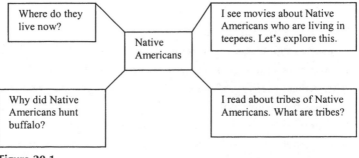

Figure 20.1.

This process assumes children will take part in the planning process as well as provide multiple opportunities for decision making and critical thinking. Students with the teacher can design exploratory situations that allow students to engage in interactive experiences.

The teacher takes on more of the role of facilitator and guide of student learning, but also provides structured experiences to teach skills students need to complete activities or projects. Students work independently at times to learn more about the topic, but they also collaborate in groups to read, investigate problems, and complete projects related to the theme or topic. Children interact and learn from each other as well as the teacher.

2. What are the key elements?

THEME: Selected with the students or a required topic of study.

FOCUS STATEMENT: One sentence that summarizes the direction and intent of the unit.

THEME WEB: Graphic of ideas and questions surrounding the theme generated with teacher and children.

ACTIVITIES AND PROJECTS: Teacher, with student input, compiles teacher-directed, teacher-child initiated, and child-initiated activities that include needed content and skills across all desired subject areas, for example, art, mathematics, reading, music, science, and social studies.

UNIT OBJECTIVES: Teacher develops desired knowledge and skills students should know or be able to do as a result of selected activities and projects.

SCHEDULING: Teacher plans whole-group and small-group lessons, activities, and field trips with student input and then schedules these throughout the week(s). Usually themes start with a "kick-off" activity and then culminate with a presentation of student projects.

FAMILY INVOLVMENT: Families can play various roles by helping to provide needed materials, present their expertise on a theme, or they can help students with parts of projects at home.

EVALUATION: During the thematic unit activities and at the end of the unit, the teacher plans and carries out formal and informal assessment of student mastery of the desired objectives.

3. How does the thematic approach differ from the project approach?

The thematic approach to teaching usually originates from ideas and activities that the teacher creates based on required standards or schoolwide grade level objectives. This may be a theme that the teacher uses every fall with a new grade level of children each year. The teacher usually lays out a one-week plan of activities that cover that theme. Some activities may be learning-center-based and other may be whole-group activities. There can be some flexibility in the theme-based activities as to when these are scheduled or the grouping of children in small-group activities. The project approach topic for child and teacher study is often derived from teacher observations of children at play and work to learn what topic may be highly motivating for these children. Children (with teacher guidance and ongoing assessment to note the direction the project should go) research concepts related to the topic that the teacher and children mutually agree upon. In the project approach, children pose questions and then conduct research to find answers to those questions. The direction the project takes is very dependent on children's level of interest and teachers' guidance rather than on a predetermined set of objectives or standards (Helm & Katz, 2001).

CONCLUSION

Teachers can always borrow theme ideas from other teachers. Recycle some of your theme activities by using these with other classes of children in future years, so you can get the most out of your investment. Do a lot of kid-watching of children at the beginning of each school year; some years the theme used in a previous year just does not fit. Swap theme activities and plans with other teachers to develop a great library that can be tapped to provide the theme that motivates each group of children. But above all, teachers can have a lot of fun right along with children as they explore new horizons together!

REFERENCES

Barton, K. C. & Smith, L. A. (2000). Themes or Motifs? Aiming for Coherence through Interdisciplinary Outline. *The Reading Teacher, 54*(1): 54–64. The authors illustrate ways to provide true thematic teaching and not just activities related to a topic.

Borich, G. D. (2000). *Effective Teaching Methods* (4th ed.). Upper Saddle River, NJ: Prentice Hall. This comprehensive text provides explanations for effective teaching methods and supports and explains the utility of thematic units.

Fredricks, A. D., Meinbach, A. M., & Rothlein, L. (2000). *Thematic Units: An Integrated Approach to Teaching Science and Social Studies* (2nd ed.). Norwood, MA: Christopher Gordon Pub, Inc. While addressing issues specific to science and social studies units, this text provides guidance for creating units that include all content areas, too.

Helm, J. H. & Katz, L. (2001). *Young Investigators: The Project Approach in the Early Years.* New York: Teachers College Press. This book thoroughly explains project work and provides guiding questions for teachers to successfully facilitate all children's learning.

Lindquest, T. & Selwyn, D. (2000). Social Studies at the Center: Integrating Kids, Content, and Literacy. Portsmouth, NH: Heinemann. The authors show how social studies' themes can be used as a focal point of learning.

Martinello, M. L. & Cook, G. E. (2000). *Interdisciplinary Inquiry in Teaching and Learning* (2nd ed.). Upper Saddle River, NJ: Prentice-Hall. The authors provide evidence for the value of interdisciplinary studies to promote inquiry.

Roberts, P. L. & Kellough, R. D. (1999). *A Guide for Developing Interdisciplinary Thematic Units* (2nd ed.). Upper Saddle River, NJ: Prentice-Hall. This book provides step-by-step instructions on how to develop culturally sensitive thematic units by integrating content and using technology tools.

Wineburg, S. & Grossman, P. (Eds.). (2000). *Interdisciplinary Curriculum: Challenges to Implementation.* New York: Teachers College Press. Contributing authors to this book blend theory with practices to share insights about schoolwide adoption of interdisciplinary instruction.

Wood, K. E. (2001). *Interdisciplinary Instruction: A Practical Guide for Elementary and Middle School Teachers.* Upper Saddle River, NJ: Prentice-Hall. Besides presenting clear steps to developing thematic instruction, this book emphasizes the thinking skills children develop as a result of working on thematic units.

Wortham, S. C. (2001). *Early Childhood Curriculum: Developmental Bases for Learning and Teaching* (3rd ed.). Upper Saddle River, NJ: Prentice-Hall. Certain types of goals and activities (i.e., block play) unique to early childhood theme-based curriculums and activities also found in elementary classes are described in chapters of the book.

Wray, D. (2001). *Inquiry in the Classroom: Creating It, Encouraging It, Enjoying It.* Portsmouth, NH: Heinemann. Teachers are shown how inquiry-based teaching and learning with projects is highly motivating.

INDEX

ABOUT THE AUTHORS

Sally C. Mayberry is a professor in the College of Education at Florida Gulf Coast University. Receiving her undergraduate degree from Randolph-Macon Woman's College, she continued on to the University of Virginia to earn her master's degree. An elementary school teacher for fifteen years, she left the classroom to earn her doctorate at the University of Miami and enter the field of higher education. At FGCU she teaches undergraduate and graduate classes in mathematics and science education and in classroom management. Her current topics of interest are inclusion, problem solving, the integrated curriculum, critical thinking, authentic assessment, and technology implementation.

A frequent presenter at national and state mathematics, science, and reading conferences, she is currently speaking on the integration of literature, mathematics, and science in the curriculum. Dr. Mayberry has authored and coauthored ten books and three articles. Two additional articles and one book are currently being reviewed by professional organizations. Entertaining a love for learning and teaching since she was a little girl, Dr. Mayberry still looks forward to weekly visits in local schools helping children learn firsthand about mathematics manipulatives and science activities with ladybugs, earthworms, and butterflies.

Lynn Hartle is an associate professor at the University of Central Florida in Orlando. Dr. Hartle received her bachelor's degree in elementary education from Grand Valley State College in Allendale, Michigan, and then received her Montessori Pre-Primary Certificate. While earning a Master of Arts in Early Childhood and Special Education from Tennessee Technological University in Cookeville, Tennessee, Lynn directed and taught in the Montessori Children's House she founded. Dr. Hartle later earned her Ph.D. in Curriculum and Instruction from The Pennsylvania State University in State College, Pennsylvania.

Her career in higher education included positions at East Stroudsburg University in Pennsylvania and the University of Florida, and she was invited as a founding faculty member at the Florida Gulf Coast University. Over the years, she has taught more than fourteen different early childhood, elementary, and early childhood special education college courses; team teaching some of those. Each class is taught with consideration of the role of technology in teaching and her research interest—teachers' emerging understandings of how to differentiate practices for diverse learners. Dr. Hartle's work has been published in various national journals and books and she is a frequent speaker at national conferences. She has also served two terms as vice president for conferences for the National Association for Early Childhood Teacher Educators.